W9-BLO-024

*God and the New Atheism*

# God and the New Atheism

## A CRITICAL RESPONSE TO DAWKINS, HARRIS, AND HITCHENS

John F. Haught

Westminster John Knox Press
LOUISVILLE • LONDON

© 2008 John F. Haught

*All rights reserved.* No part of this book may be reproduced or transmitted in any form or by any means, electronic or mechanical, including photocopying, recording, or by any information storage or retrieval system, without permission in writing from the publisher. For information, address Westminster John Knox Press, 100 Witherspoon Street, Louisville, Kentucky 40202-1396.

*Book design by Drew Stevens*
*Cover design by designpointinc.com*

*First edition*
Published by Westminster John Knox Press
Louisville, Kentucky

This book is printed on acid-free paper that meets the American National Standards Institute Z39.48 standard. ∞

PRINTED IN THE UNITED STATES OF AMERICA

08 09 10 11 12 13 14 15 16 17 — 10 9 8 7 6 5 4 3 2 1

**Library of Congress Cataloging-in-Publication Data**

Haught, John F.
    God and the new atheism : a critical response to Dawkins, Harris, and Hitchens / John F. Haught.—1st ed.
        p. cm.
    Includes bibliographical references and index.
    ISBN 978-0-664-23304-4 (alk. paper)
    1. Atheism.  2. Dawkins, Richard, 1941—Religion.  3. Harris, Sam, 1967—Religion.  4. Hitchens, Christopher—Religion.  I. Title.
BL2747.3.H378 2008
211'.80922—dc22

                                              2007041718

# Contents

# Preface

The popular press and Internet discussions have brought considerable attention to the recent atheistic declarations of Richard Dawkins, Sam Harris, and Christopher Hitchens, but they have seldom looked very far into the background assumptions of these authors. I have attempted to do so here, and my hope is that the following pages will provide readers of many backgrounds, interests, and persuasions a compact set of reflections that will prove helpful and interesting in the never-ending discussion of religious belief and modern skepticism.

I want to thank Westminster John Knox Press for the opportunity to write this succinct critique of the "new atheism." I am especially grateful to Philip Law for the invitation to put down these thoughts, for his most skillful assistance from start to finish, and for the many substantive suggestions he has offered for making the book readable to a wide audience. It has been a most pleasant experience working with him on this project. Thanks also to Daniel Braden as well as to Tom King and Kathleen Rottenborn for reading the manuscript and offering helpful suggestions. Most of all, thanks to my wife, Evelyn, for her generous encouragement and always wise editorial advice.

# Introduction

Anyone who keeps track of what sells well these days in the world of publishing cannot fail to have noticed the recent outbreak of provocative atheistic treatises. Best-selling books by Richard Dawkins, Sam Harris, and Christopher Hitchens have drawn an extraordinary amount of attention. Many readers, including some academics, have found these books not only interesting but also, in some cases, convincing. Dawkins's *The God Delusion* says extremely well, though not always accurately, what some scientists and philosophers have already been thinking. Likewise Harris, in *The End of Faith* and *Letter to a Christian Nation,* and Hitchens, in *God Is Not Great: How Religion Poisons Everything,* have stated clearly and entertainingly what many of their readers also consider to be wrong with religion. I shall refer to these works collectively as the "new atheism."[1]

A number of other intellectually comparable books are now trying in the name of science to debunk religion and especially the idea of God.[2] I was initially tempted to include Daniel Dennett's *Breaking the Spell: Religion as a Natural Phenomenon* more focally in my survey of the new atheism, but Dennett's book is an unnecessarily lengthy argument for a relatively simple, and by no means exceptional way of assaulting religion.[3] Moreover, in responding to the three books I have chosen to evaluate, I am in effect also addressing Dennett's chief claim, namely, that religion should be studied naturalistically, especially in terms of evolutionary biology. Dennett's name will come up often enough anyway, but because of constraints on this book's length and intricacy, I have decided to deal most explicitly with the other three authors, and with Dennett more occasionally.

Dennett's main point is that evolutionary biology provides the deepest explanation of all living phenomena, including ethics and religion. Looking for an evolutionary understanding of religion, I shall argue, is theologically unobjectionable. In fact, theology, as I understand it, has no objection to pushing evolutionary explanations of all living systems, including religions, as far as it is logically possible and scientifically fruitful to do so. To science, after all, religions are as much a part of nature as all other observable realities. However, Dennett does not stop with the acknowledgment that religion is a natural phenomenon that science has every right to study. For him, as for Dawkins, a naturalistic understanding of religion leaves no meaningful room at all for plausible theological accounts of why most people are religious. Theology for Dennett, as for Dawkins, Harris, and Hitchens, is now completely superfluous. Science alone can tell us what religion is really all about, and it can provide better answers than theology to every important question people ask. According to Dawkins, science is even qualified to decide whether or not God exists. Although Dennett is not quite that self-assured, he shares the belief that science's cognitional sweep is exhaustive, and hence that it leaves no meaningful space for a theological explanation of religion.

Dennett's belief that science can provide an adequate understanding of religion is obviously not a scientifically proven or even provable claim. It is a dogma, a declaration of faith. No massive accumulation of sarcastic putdowns or intellectual gymnastics can conceal this fact from the critical reader. The belief system that Dennett and the other new atheists subscribe to is known as "scientific naturalism." Its central dogma is that only nature, including humans and our creations, is real; that God does not exist; and that science alone can give us complete and reliable knowledge of reality. Since God does not fall within the realm of "evidence" that science deals with, any reasonable, scientifically educated person must therefore repudiate belief in God. Since almost everything Dennett writes about religion is based on his own belief in scientific naturalism, I shall be responding critically to his writings even if I do not always mention him by name.

According to Dawkins and Dennett, one must decide between theological and Darwinian explanations. Each reader must choose one rather than the other. It cannot be both. In issuing this dogma Dennett and Dawkins are simply restating one of the central assumptions of almost all science-inspired atheism. Carl Sagan, Michael Shermer, Steven Weinberg, Owen Flanagan, and Victor Stenger, just to name a few, have made similar claims,[4] so there is no need here to make a separate study of these writers. The authors I examine cover the same territory and more anyway. Numerous other current books, articles, and reviews subscribe to the central tenets of the new atheism, but I have seen little in these other works that has not been said as well, if not better, by the three authors I highlight in this volume.

I must confess, however, my disappointment in witnessing the recent surge of interest in atheism. It's not that my livelihood as a theologian is remotely at stake—although the authors in question would fervently wish that it were so. Nor is it that the treatment of religion in these tracts consists mostly of breezy overgeneralizations that leave out almost everything that theologians would want to highlight in their own contemporary discussion of God. Rather, the new atheism is so theologically unchallenging. Its engagement with theology lies at about the same level of reflection on faith that one can find in contemporary creationist and fundamentalist literature. This is not surprising since it is from creationists and intelligent design theists that the new atheists seem to have garnered much of their understanding of religious faith. Mainline theologians, as well as students of intellectual history, will find in these publications very little that they have not seen before. Nevertheless, I can assume that many readers of this book will not have the theological background to know quite how to deal with them, and so it is not only for specialists, teachers, and students, but also for the general reading public that I offer in these pages a theological response.

By using the term "theological" here I mean to indicate, first of all, that my reflections arise out of my belonging to a theistic religious tradition, that is, one that professes belief in a personal God, a God of infinite power and love, who creates and sustains the world, and who forever opens up the world to a new and unprecedented future, a God who makes all things new. This essentially biblical understanding of God holds that the divine mystery can be approached only by way of faith, trust, and hope (which are almost indistinguishable concepts in biblical literature), not as a present cognitive or religious possession. Nevertheless, even though God cannot be known apart from faith and hope, most theology allows that faith and hope are entirely consistent with and fully supportive of human reason, including its pursuit of scientific understanding.

Second, theology, as I use the term, is an appreciative but also critical, philosophical reflection on religions that profess belief in God. When I refer to "theology" henceforth, I employ this term as a general label for the work of many biblically informed, critically reflective, religious thinkers whom I have found to be helpful in shaping my own understanding of faith and atheism. Specifically, I mean thinkers such as Paul Tillich, Alfred North Whitehead, Paul Ricoeur, Rudolf Bultmann, Edward Schillebeeckx, Bernard Lonergan, Karl Barth, John Bowker, Elizabeth Johnson, Karl Rahner, Jürgen Moltmann, Wolfhart Pannenberg, Ian Barbour, David Tracy, Dorothee Soelle, Sallie McFague, Henri de Lubac, Hans Jonas, Emil Fackenheim, and Seyyed Hossein Nasr, just to mention a handful.

Clearly the new atheists are not familiar with any of these religious thinkers, and the hostility to what they call "theology" has almost nothing to do with theology as I use the term. Occasionally our critics come close to suspecting that there may be a whole other world of relevant religious thought out there, but they want to make things easy for themselves and their readers, so they keep theology, at least in my sense of the term, out of their discussion altogether. Their strategy is to suppress in effect any significant theological voices that might wish to join in conversation with them. As a result of this exclusion, the intellectual quality of their atheism is unnecessarily diminished. Their understanding of religious faith remains consistently at the same unscholarly level as the unreflective, superstitious, and literalist religiosity of those they criticize. Moreover, amid all their justified outrage at religious abuses, they cannot fathom the possibility that folk religion also often rises to heights of nobility, courage, and authenticity that no fair and objective scholarship should ignore.

Ideally the authors of the books I shall be evaluating will also peek into the following pages, but since their own writings so far show no interest in theology, it is probably too much to expect that they would wish to tune in now. I should also be pleased if Jewish and Muslim theists would find something of interest in this study, although they certainly have their own unique responses to the new atheism.

## WHY THIS BOOK?

I have decided to write the present book in order to expose the fundamental flaws and fallacies that make the new atheism much less impressive than it may initially seem to be. I cannot treat each author in detail, nor respond to every point, but it is not necessary to do so in order to expose their shared inconsistencies. The new atheists have so much in common with one another as well as with earlier kinds of atheism that what I shall have to say in criticism of one, apart from some minor discrepancies, generally applies to the others as well. This conclusion is especially true of the worldview they share with many scientists, philosophers, and other contemporary intellectuals. I am referring here to the increasingly influential vision of reality that I earlier called scientific naturalism. Because of its importance in shaping the mind-set of all the new atheists, including many whom I am not able to mention, I shall list here its main tenets:

1. Apart from nature, which includes human beings and our cultural creations, there is nothing. There is no God, no soul, and no life beyond death.

2. Nature is self-originating, not the creation of God.
3. The universe has no overall point or purpose, although individual human lives can be lived purposefully.
4. Since God does not exist, all explanations and all causes are purely natural and can be understood only by science.
5. All the various features of living beings, including human intelligence and behavior, can be explained ultimately in purely natural terms, and today this usually means in evolutionary, specifically Darwinian, terms.

To these tenets of scientific naturalism, the new atheists would add the following:

6. Faith in God is the cause of innumerable evils and should be rejected on moral grounds.
7. Morality does not require belief in God, and people behave better without faith than with it.

These shared assumptions, the intellectual foundation of the new atheism, require a response if we are to get to its roots. In a previous book, *Is Nature Enough? Meaning and Truth in the Age of Science,* I have argued at much more length that scientific naturalism is an incoherent and self-subverting belief system, but I cannot repeat the whole argument in this briefer discussion. I mention the earlier, and much more academic, work in case some readers are looking for a considerably amplified version of some of the criticisms I present here as they apply to Dawkins, Harris, and Hitchens.

I proceed as follows: In chapter 1 I ask just how new the new atheism is. In this first chapter I intend to provide a brief summary of the claims of each of our three authors, asking if any features might merit special consideration. I observe that the works under study provide a fresh and sometimes entertaining exposition of important issues, but they are essentially the same as those that have preoccupied religions and theologies for generations. Five persistent questions naturally arise in any discussion of atheism, and these serve as the topics for chapters 3–7: Does theology matter (chapter 3)? Is God a "hypothesis" that science can confirm or reject (chapter 4)? Why are people inclined toward religious belief at all (chapter 5)? Can we be good without God (chapter 6)? Is the idea of a personal God believable in an age of science (chapter 7)?

Chapter 2 asks just how atheistic the new atheism is. What would a Nietzsche, Camus, or Sartre think of Dawkins, Harris, and Hitchens? Here I distinguish between the "hard-core" atheism of several classic critics of religion on the one hand, and the new "soft-core" variety characteristic of our new atheists on the other. Then I ask how well the latter measures up to the rigorous standards of the former. Finally, in chapter 8 I offer a specifically Christian response to the questions treated in chapters 3–7. For some readers this last chapter will be seen as optional, even though for me personally it is the most important. My first seven chapters avoid approaching the new atheism from an exclusively Christian point of view. Instead, my critique is styled in such a way that non-Christian theists (especially Jewish and Muslim believers in God), as well as atheists and agnostics can easily follow along. Only in the concluding chapter do I sketch a Christian theological response. I show in chapter 8 that what our new atheists understand by "God" has almost nothing to do with what Christian faith and theology today understand by that name.

The deeper I became involved in the writing of this book, the more evident it became to me that I was offering a critique not only of the new atheism but also of the kind of religious thought, ethics, and spirituality against which it is reacting. I suggest that there are reliable and more interesting theological alternatives to both. However, even though the new atheists reject the God of creationists, fundamentalists, terrorists, and intelligent design (ID) advocates, it is not without interest that they have decided to debate with these extremists rather than with any major theologians. This choice of antagonists betrays their unconscious privileging of literalist and conservative versions of religious thought over the more traditionally mainstream types—which they completely ignore and implicitly reject for their unorthodoxy. The new atheists are saying in effect that if God exists at all, we should allow this God's identity to be determined once and for all by the fundamentalists of the Abrahamic religious traditions. I believe they have chosen this strategy not only to make their job of demolition easier, but also because they have a barely disguised admiration for the simplicity of their opponents' views of reality. The best evidence of their own attraction to an uncomplicated worldview can be found in their allegiance to the even simpler assumptions of scientific naturalism.

# 1

## How New Is the New Atheism?

"When the Son of Man comes, will he find faith on earth?"
—Luke 18:8

The day after the World Trade Center's twin towers came down in September 2001, my wife and I attended a special service at Holy Trinity Catholic Church near Georgetown University where I had been teaching for many years. Bill Byron, the Jesuit pastor and former president of the Catholic University of America, celebrated Mass and delivered a prayerful homily. If you want peace, he said, practice justice. People of faith should never give up their hope for improving the quality of life all over the world. We need to avoid simplistic solutions and blanket condemnation of religions. We must all work for a more just world no matter how long it takes, and without the use of violence. Amid the enormous shock and grief in the aftermath of 9/11, a similar encouragement to practice tolerance, love, and justice pealed through places of worship all over the world.

Around the same time these services were going on, a young Stanford University philosopher and student of neuroscience named Sam Harris was devising another, much more radical solution to the escalating problem of worldwide terrorism. Tolerance and compassion simply will not work, he thought.

1

Indeed, tolerance of faith is a major cause of the problem. Harris's proposal, as presented in his best-selling books *The End of Faith* and *Letter to a Christian Nation,* is crystal clear.[1] We can rid the world of faith not by violence but by reason and the spread of science. Envisioning himself almost as a new Buddha, Harris resolved to share with his readers—and with the whole world—something like a new version of the ancient Buddha's Four Noble Truths. Richard Dawkins and Christopher Hitchens make essentially the same set of claims.

## THE FIRST EVIDENT TRUTH

Many people in the world are living needlessly miserable lives, Harris notes, faintly echoing the Buddha's First Noble Truth that "all life is suffering." Harris's background assumption is that the purpose of human life is to find happiness. In contrast, the philosopher Immanuel Kant and other wise thinkers and spiritual masters have taught that happiness can come only as a by-product of the search for something eternal. Aiming for happiness directly is a sure way not to find it. However, if God does not exist and the universe is purposeless, the best we can do is strive for a world in which happiness, "a form of well-being that supersedes all others," is ensured for the greatest number of individuals (Harris 205).[2] Harris does not define happiness, nor does he distinguish it from other kinds of gratification. He simply assumes that we all know intuitively what happiness is and that we should make it the goal of all ethical existence (170–71).

That we all suffer and eventually die is inevitable, Harris realizes, because that's how nature and evolution work. We can alleviate some natural afflictions and lengthen our lives even if we cannot eliminate pain completely. However, the senseless suffering that terrorism causes is another matter. Maybe we *can* do something about that, something radical. As with the Buddha's first realization, we must begin by facing up fully to the fact that the actual world features a great deal of unnecessary wretchedness, most notably such events as the 9/11 massacre.

## THE SECOND EVIDENT TRUTH

The cause of so much unnecessary distress, Harris declares, is faith, particularly in the form of belief in God. Faith is "belief without evidence" (58–73, 85), and for Hitchens this is what "poisons everything." Dawkins agrees (308), and all three authors try to convince their readers that the monotheistic faiths—Judaism, Christianity, and Islam—underlie a sizable portion of the evils human beings have afflicted on one another throughout the last three millennia. But it is not just horrifying ideas of God such as those of al-Qaeda and other fanatics that cause so much unnecessary pain. It is faith, pure and simple.[3]

This claim is not quite the same as the Buddha's Second Noble Truth, which states that the cause of suffering is greedy desire (*tanha*). But there is a resemblance, since faith too seems to be an inexhaustible craving, in this case for insane ideas to satisfy the seemingly bottomless appetite so many humans have for delusions (Harris 23, 26–27, 38–39, 58–73). In a formula almost as compact as the Buddha's—the cause of suffering is faith—our new atheists want to focus our attention on exactly what needs to be eradicated if true happiness is to be realized.

The idea of God fabricated by faith is "*intrinsically* dangerous" (44) and morally evil, no matter what form it takes in our imaginations. Why? Because there is no *evidence* for it, and in fact "no evidence is even *conceivable*" (23). Basing knowledge on "evidence" is not only cognitionally necessary but morally essential as well. By failing the test of evidence that makes science reliable, "religious faith represents so uncompromising a misuse of the power of our minds that it forms a kind of perverse, cultural singularity—a vanishing point beyond which rational discourse proves impossible. When foisted upon each generation anew, it renders us incapable of realizing just how much of our world has been unnecessarily ceded to a dark and barbarous past" (25).

The new atheists want to make it very clear that what is so evil about the God religions is not only the crude anthropomorphic images of deity that arise from our "baser natures—forces like greed, hatred, and fear" (15), but also that they arise from "faith" rather than from "evidence." Both "faith" and "evidence" need to be understood carefully. Here the term "faith" functions for the new atheists almost as "greedy desire" does for the Buddha. The Buddha had attributed our suffering to our tendency to cling to things so obsessively that we set ourselves up for disappointment whenever we have to face the transience of all beings. So if we want happiness it would be better not to cling to anything at all. For the Buddha, "greedy desire" is the source of our suffering. For the new atheists it is our tendency to believe in *anything* without evidence. Faith makes the world so much more miserable than it needs to be.

Belief in God is an especially noxious version of faith. Just consider all the ways in which belief in God and the afterlife are messing up the world today. I am writing this page, for example, on the most deadly day to date of the Iraq fiasco (August 15, 2007), when Muslim extremists slaughtered as many as five hundred members of the Yazidi sect. Blindly believing improbable propositions concerning God and the afterlife, a band of religious believers blew themselves up in the name of God in order to blow up other religious believers at the same time. What more proof do we need that theistic faith is not only deluded but also dangerous? Faith in God may seem innocent to most of us, but according to Harris, faith can lead to anything. The foolish credulity that leads Christians to believe, in Harris's words, that Jesus "cheated death, and rose bodily into the heavens," or the preposterous idea of transubstantiation that allows Catholics to believe that Jesus can be "eaten in the form of a cracker" and that the faithful can drink his blood by virtue of "a few Latin words spoken over your favorite Burgundy," may seem harmless enough (73). But the opening that faith makes for such innocent nonsense unfortunately also provides the space for unjustified beliefs that lead to "the most monstrous crimes against humanity" (78–79).

The new atheists define faith as belief without evidence. "Evidence" is a crucial term, showing up innumerable times in Harris's book and at key points in Dawkins's (282–83). But what is "evidence"? The authors never carefully define what they mean by the term, but it is clear that it signifies for them whatever is scientifically testable, empirically available, or publicly observable. Extraordinary claims such as those of religion, as Harris asserts, require an "extraordinary kind of testing," but none is available (41). Since science alone can reliably verify or falsify human propositions, one must conclude that religious ideas, lacking any physical evidence as they do, cannot legitimately claim to be truthful. Without passing through some kind of empirical testing, almost anything could become admissible in the religious mind, including the belief that martyrdom by suicide bombing will launch one immediately into paradise. So, only claims for which there is "sufficient evidence" are acceptable to those who want an end to human misery.

Theologians today understand faith as the commitment of one's whole being to God. But the new atheists, echoing a now-obsolete theology, think of faith in a narrow intellectual and propositional sense. The seat of faith for them is not a vulnerable heart but a weak intellect. Harris, Dawkins, and Hitchens consider all forms of faith to be irrational, and abusing reason by harboring faith in one's mind is shockingly unethical as well. It is morally wrong to believe anything without sufficient evidence. In this respect the new atheists adopt what an older generation of atheists called the "ethic of knowledge" as the foundation of both moral and cognitional life. In the late 1960s the noted biochemist and atheist Jacques Monod claimed that the "ethic of knowledge" must be the foundation of all moral and intellectual claims. He declared that it is unethical to accept any ideas that fail to adhere to the "postulate of objectivity." In other words it is morally wrong to accept any claims that cannot be verified in principle by "objective" scientific knowing. But, then, what about that precept itself? Can anyone prove objectively that the postulate of objectivity is true? Here Monod was much more honest than the new atheists. He admitted that an exception must be made for the postulate of objectivity. The ethic of knowledge is itself an "arbitrary" choice, not a claim for which there could ever be sufficient scientific evidence. Faith, it seems, makes an opening wide enough for atheism too.[4]

Of course, all knowing has to start somewhere, and that somewhere is rightly called faith, even if our critics are offended by the term. At some foundational level all knowing is rooted in a declaration of trust, in a "will to believe." For example, we have to trust that the universe makes some kind of sense before we can even begin the search for its intelligibility. Unacknowledged declarations of faith underlie every claim the atheist makes as well, including the formal repudiation of faith. In a classic essay entitled "The Will to Believe," which our atheists show no sign of ever having read, the philosopher William James took W. K. Clifford to task for issuing so arbitrarily the ethical proclamation that it is always wrong to believe anything without sufficient evidence.[5] All you have to do is read James's very important essay to observe that, at least in what we have seen so far, there is absolutely nothing new in the new atheism. But let us keep looking.

## THE THIRD EVIDENT TRUTH

The way to avoid unnecessary human suffering today is to abolish faith from the face of the earth. The Buddha's Third Noble Truth states that the way to overcome suffering is to find release from clinging desire. The new atheists—especially Harris, who favors a very highly edited version of Buddhism—believe that release from bondage to faith can help rid the world of unnecessary suffering. Here "faith" is the bottomless cave in consciousness that gives domicile to everything from belief in UFOs, to witches, souls, angels, devils, paradise, and God. Most of these beliefs seem harmless enough, but if we allow people to get away with even the most innocuous instances of faith, what is to prevent a Muslim radical from believing that God's will is the destruction of Israel and the United States, or a Zionist from believing that God wants us to murder innocent Palestinians, or a Christian from believing that it is God's will to bomb abortion clinics? Once God's will is fancied to favor such acts of violence, then anything is possible—including the most unthinkable horrors.

Understandably, then, the new atheists ask how we can bring about a world where indiscriminate killing and maiming in the name of God become truly unthinkable. Since such a world does not yet exist, a radical solution is required: we must get rid of faith altogether. Everyone needs to just stop believing in any assertion that cannot be backed up by "evidence." This applies especially to all the books that religious people have held holy for ages. Since the allegedly inspired literature of the God religions is a product of faith, there is no reason to take it seriously. Aside from an aesthetically appealing passage here and there, the Scriptures of all religions are worthless. Furthermore, whatever seems morally right or aesthetically charming in our allegedly sacred books and traditions could have been arrived at by reason operating independently of faith.

This censuring of faith applies also to theology, which the new atheists hold in utter contempt, aghast at the fact that in our day and age there are even such absurdities as academic departments with that name. They wonder why more scholars and other people whom we expect to be smart do not seem to notice how dangerous theology is to the world. Theology, after all, leads one Muslim faction to slaughter another in the name of God. It is in the heads of theologians that incentives for inquisitions and massacres are hatched. The evidence is undeniable. The history of Judaism, Christianity, and Islam is a trail of untold suffering and death engendered by ridiculous theological disputes. Such is the judgment of all three of our critics. Look honestly at the root of today's terrorism, they would advise us. Look at all the national and international problems caused by ideas of God that arise from theological fantasies that feed on our pathetic propensity for faith. Every time you remove your shoes at your airport's security control, one might add, just reflect on the ultimate cause of this nuisance as well.

The unprecedented dangers that threaten us today, Harris insists, will only get worse unless a drastic solution can be found. Liberals and socialists naively suggest that if we want peace we all need to practice justice. But such a solution is not extreme enough for the new atheists. The root cause of the most insane forms of violence is not poverty and injustice anyway. Rather, it is faith and theology. Faith and theology may lead some people to prayerful services such as the one I mentioned at the beginning of this chapter. But since prayer is based on the irrationality of faith, by worshiping God we are only perpetuating the suffering of humanity in the long run. The day after 9/11, instead of participating in a religious service, my wife and I would have made better use of our time, according to Harris, by working toward a radical secularism that denies any status to faith of any sort. Only "the end of faith" holds any promise for saving the world.

Rather than embracing the ancient Buddha's milder Third Noble Truth as the way to end suffering, the new atheists seek to initiate us into a radically different but, they think, more effective kind of asceticism—namely, cleansing our minds of faith. This new discipline of purification, if executed according to the new atheists' severe standards, will lead to the suppression of all childish inclinations to believe without evidence. The idea of God must therefore be erased forever from human awareness, but this cannot take place apart from the "end of faith." Cleansing the world of the likes of Osama bin Laden and al-Qaeda by force is not going to do the job. What needs eliminating is faith in every form, and our new atheists all think of themselves as pioneering this unprecedented purge.

At this point our debunkers might seem to be finished, but they are just getting started. Here they begin offering something startlingly new, at least outside the reach of atheistic dictatorships. It is not just faith, they say, but our polite and civil tolerance of faith that must be uprooted if progress toward true happiness is to be made. Harris is most explicit on this point. Religious moderates and their defense of the right to faith, he fumes, are, "in large part, responsible for the religious conflict in our world . . ." (45). Dawkins fully supports him:

As long as we respect the principle that religious faith must be respected simply because it is religious faith it is hard to withhold respect from the faith of Osama bin Laden and the suicide bombers. The alternative, one so transparent that it should need no urging, is to abandon the principle of automatic respect for religious faith. This is one reason I do everything in my power to warn people against faith itself, not just against so-called "extremist" faith. The teachings of "moderate" religion, though not extremist in themselves, are an open invitation to extremism. (306)

Tolerance of faith remains an unquestioned part of democratic societies, but the evil illusions that this forbearance allows will continue to cause untold misery. If we indulge any kind of faith at all we set ourselves up for victimization by "true believers" of all sorts. Indiscriminate respect for faith is enough to make each tolerant soul among us a de facto accomplice in evil.

Instead of compromising with religious faith in the genteel way that secular and religious moderates have done in the past, the new atheists want us to abandon any such respect for freedom of faith and religious thought altogether. Nothing impedes a clear-sighted grasp of the world's most urgent problem today—religiously inspired terrorism—more thoughtlessly than moderate theology and liberal secular tolerance of faith. We must realize at last that our theological, secular, leftist, postmodern, and simply good-mannered tolerance of faith has become intolerable itself. Religious moderates, Harris writes, "imagine that the path to peace will be paved once each of us has learned to respect the unjustified beliefs of others." But the "very idea of religious tolerance—born of the notion that every human being should be free to believe whatever he wants about God—is one of the principal forces driving us toward the abyss" (14–15). Abjuring any concern for political correctness, Harris seems deadly serious in his proclamation that we can no longer tolerate the liberal tolerance of faith. Here, then, we meet something fairly new in the writings of the new atheists.

Also new in Dawkins, Harris, and Hitchens is an intolerance not only of theology but also of the soft, "Neville Cham-
berlain" accommodation that most of their fellow atheists and
scientific naturalists have made toward the existence of faith
(Dawkins 66–69). In many years of studying and conversing
with scientific naturalists I have yet to encounter such a sweep-
ing intolerance of tolerance. Intolerance of tolerance seems to
be a truly novel feature of the new atheists' solution to the
problem of human misery. Nearly everything else that Dawkins,
Harris, and Hitchens (and their philosophical mentor Dennett) have to say about religion, faith, and theology has been
said already. Certainly their blanket rejection of religious
faith's cognitional standing is not new, nor is their indictment
of religion on moral grounds. Scientific naturalism, in whose
tenets our new atheists have been methodically schooled, has
long held that nature is all there is and that science is the
privileged road to understanding the world. However, most
devotees of scientific naturalism in the modern period have rec-
ognized that they are fortunate to live in cultures and countries
where a plurality of faiths is accepted. They have been grateful
for this leniency, since otherwise scientific naturalism may
never have been allowed to exist alongside belief systems that
are ideologically opposed to it. In fact, if it were up to a vote in
the United States today, as the new atheists would surely agree,
scientific naturalism would be voted off the map by a majority
of citizens.

The new atheists are right in pointing out how so many
other belief systems than their own are often intolerant and
barbaric. But surely they must realize that their own belief system, scientific naturalism, would never have established itself
in the modern world were it not for the tolerance extended to
"freethinkers" by the same religious cultures that gave rise to
science. Their reply is that religious cultures themselves never
had any real moral or rational justification for existing in the
first place. Faith, since it is intrinsically evil, should ideally
never have been tendered any right to exist at all. Furthermore,
when human intelligence first emerged in evolution it should

never have allowed itself to be taken captive by faith, no matter how biologically adaptive this alliance of mind with unreason happened to be.

Harris thinks he can get by with this extreme intolerance since as far as he is concerned it is based on reason rather than faith. However, Harris's and Dawkins's own scientism, the intellectual backbone of their scientific naturalism, is a belief for which there can be no "sufficient" scientific or empirical "evidence" either. There is no way, without circular thinking, to set up a scientific experiment to demonstrate that every true proposition must be based in empirical evidence rather than faith. The censuring of every instance of faith, in the narrow new atheist sense of the term, would have to include the suppression of scientism also. The truly thoughtful scientific naturalists—Einstein is a good example—have been honest enough to admit that faith, especially faith that the universe is comprehensible at all, is essential to ground the work of science itself. Moreover, the claim that truth can be attained only by reason and science functioning independently of any faith is itself a faith claim. Complete consistency would require that the new atheists' world of thought be cleansed of scientism and scientific naturalism as well.

## THE FOURTH EVIDENT TRUTH

The way to eliminate faith, and hence to get rid of suffering, is to follow the hallowed path of the scientific method. Issued by Harris, and endorsed by the other new atheists, this difficult but indispensable route to true enlightenment is the new atheists' version of the Eightfold Path as prescribed by the Buddha's Fourth Noble Truth. Following the path of science will give people a new kind of "right association"—namely, with those who have caught the spirit of science—and "right understanding," an empirical method that will take our minds far beyond the fantasies and banalities of religious faith. We can find true enlightenment only if we apprentice ourselves to those masters,

Harris, Dawkins, Dennett, and Hitchens among them, who have reached enlightenment by way of scientific reason.

This solution is matched in its shallowness only by the religious fundamentalism it mirrors even while opposing it. In a messy and uncertain world the appeal of a single, simple solution can be irresistible. When things turn sour it is tempting to demonize and rip out one of the countless strands in the complex web of human life, blaming everything on it alone. For example, some devout American Christians today locate the single main cause of all the ills of modernity in "Darwinism." Get rid of Darwinism, as they call it, and everything will get better. Charles Darwin, the modest naturalist from Downe, is now often identified by many Christians as the sole or main cause of our social and ethical misery. Darwin's novel ideas are held to be the ultimate cause of atheism, Nazism, Communism, and the breakdown of religion and family values. Thus, intelligent design proponent Phillip Johnson's solution to these ills is to get Darwinism out of the minds of people, and the way to do that is to begin by presenting alternatives to evolutionary theory in the public schools.[6]

Faith, for the new atheist, is the equivalent of what Darwinism is to the creationist. Get rid of faith and everything will get better. For Dawkins, Harris, and Hitchens, the banishing of faith from our minds and public life is the panacea that will end suffering and evil, at least so far as nature allows it. And the best way to dispose of faith is not by violence or even political action, but by filling minds with science and reason. Our atheist friends firmly *believe* in the effectiveness of this program. So maybe there will still be at least one instance of faith left on the earth when the Son of Man returns.

## THE MEANING OF FAITH

If it is not yet clear to the reader, the understanding of "faith" that the new atheists take for granted bears very little resemblance to that of theology. The main difference is that the new atheists think of faith as an *intellectually* erroneous attempt at something like scientific understanding, whereas theology thinks of faith as a state of self-surrender in which one's whole being, and not just the intellect, is experienced as being carried away into a dimension of reality that is much deeper and more real than anything that could be grasped by science and reason. This is why faith is so often accompanied by ritual. But the definition of faith that Dawkins, Dennett, Harris, and Hitchens all embrace is "belief without evidence." They think of faith as a set of hypotheses—such as the God hypothesis or the soul hypothesis—that lack sufficient scientific or empirical evidence for reasonable people to accept. They allow that if the right kind of empirical evidence ever turns up, then reasonable people will be permitted to give assent to the God hypothesis or the soul hypothesis. But then there will no longer be any need for faith. Knowledge will have replaced it.

For theology, however, the objective is to deepen faith, not eliminate it. In theistic traditions the essence of the ideal life, even the heroic life, is being willing to wait in faith, trust, and hope for ultimate fulfillment and final liberation. Consequently, when Harris and the others invite people to give up their faith and live only by reason, they have no idea what they are asking. The invitation to join them in a world without faith will sound to most people like a petition to shrink our world to the point where we can all be suffocated. For even if the universe contains 300 billion galaxies, and the multiverse, if it exists, billions more, educated people know that the world is still finite and perishable. And by anybody's mathematics an infinite divine mystery is still more impressive than any finite spatial and temporal magnitude at science's command. Advising people to give up what they take to be—whether rightly or wrongly—their lifeline to the infinite greatness of a divine mystery, and inviting them to squeeze their lives, minds, and hearts into the comparatively minuscule world of scientific objectification, is not going to be met with enthusiasm all around. There is nothing wrong with science, of course. But, if we may be permitted to adapt Edwin Abbott's timeless imagery, Harris, Dennett, Hitchens, and Dawkins seem like the inhabitants of a two-dimensional world who, having mastered that sphere of being, are now busy inviting those who occupy the admittedly more disorienting world of many dimensions to please come down and live with them in Flatland.[7]

# 2

# *How Atheistic Is the New Atheism?*

If anyone has written a book more critical of religious faith
than I have, I'm not aware of it.

—Sam Harris[1]

For many years I taught an introductory theology course entitled "The Problem of God" to Georgetown University undergraduates. It was always a challenge to make out a suitable
reading list for this important academic experience, but my fellow instructors and I were convinced that our students should
be exposed to the most erudite of the unbelievers. Our rationale was that any mature commitment that intelligent young
people might make to a religious faith, if they so chose, should
be critically tested by the very best opponents. The course was
at times troubling to some students and especially to the rare
youngsters who came from creationist backgrounds or whose
previous religious education had not dealt frankly with the natural sciences. But it was also an eye-opening course for students
from nonreligious and atheistic backgrounds. They had to go
through the process of learning that religion is infinitely more
nuanced than they had ever imagined. Additionally, they
would be exposed to theologies that would be much more dev-
astating in their criticism of the demonic and barbaric aspects
of human religiosity than any of the new atheists are.

I cannot speak for other college professors today, but in my own classes the new books by Dawkins, Harris, and Hitchens would never have made the list of required readings. These tirades would simply reinforce students' ignorance not only of religion, but ironically also of atheism. At best the new atheistic expositions would have been useful material for outside reading, group projects, or class presentations. And the point of these peripheral exercises would not have been to provide anything in the way of an increase of wisdom and knowledge. Rather, it would have been to see how well the relatively light fare the new atheists serve up compares with the gravity of an older and much more thoughtful generation of religious critics.

The most original "new" insight in Hitchens's book, for example, is that "religion is man-made" (8, 10, 17, 52, 54, 99–100, 115, 130, 151, 156, 167–68, 181, 202, 229, 240). This refrain rattles through the pages of his critique with all the force of a startling revelation. My students would have found it interesting, to say the least, that such a hackneyed insight would be the organizing center of a best-selling new book. After coping with the science-inspired atheism of Sigmund Freud or Bertrand Russell and the humanistic idealism of Ludwig Feuerbach and Karl Marx, the new atheism would have appeared rather haggard since it provides little in the way of a new understanding of why religion can be so dangerous.

As far as enhancing knowledge of religion is concerned, the new atheists do little more than provide a fresh catalog of the evils wrought by members of the theistic faiths. Meanwhile, truly inquisitive young minds remain restless for deeper insight. Even Freud's theory of religion's origin, along with those of Feuerbach and Marx, no matter how flawed it may have seemed to my students, at least held their attention and started them thinking about whether the whole business of religion might be an illusory human creation. In comparison with the old masters of the projection theory my students would have found Hitchens's book rather tame stuff. For while Feuerbach, Marx, and Freud provide interesting theoretical frameworks for their theories, Hitchens provides nothing of the sort.

On the other hand, I suspect that my students would have been titillated by the recent writings of Dawkins, Dennett, and others who profess to give a biological, evolutionary explanation of why people believe in God. They would have learned in our course that there is no good theological reason to object to any scientific attempts to understand religion, even in evolutionary terms. The course would have made it clear that religion can and indeed should be studied as a natural phenomenon. After all, this is the only way science can study anything, and its insights are completely compatible with any good theology. But for reasons I expand on in chapters 5 and 6, my students would have rightly wondered whether evolutionary theory, or any natural or social science, can give a complete and adequate understanding of religion. During our one-semester course students would already have encountered in Freud's book *The Future of an Illusion* the claim that science alone is a reliable road to true understanding of anything. And they would have learned from other readings that this claim is a profession of faith known as *scientism*, a modern belief system that has the additional mark of being self-contradictory.

Why self-contradictory? Because scientism tells us to take nothing on faith, and yet faith is required to accept scientism. What is remarkable is that none of the new atheists seems remotely prepared to admit that his scientism is a self-sabotaging confession of faith. Listen to Hitchens: "If one must have faith in order to believe in something, then the likelihood of that something having any truth or value is considerably diminished" (71). But this statement invalidates itself since it too arises out of faith in things unseen. There is no set of tangible experiments or visible demonstrations that could ever scientifically prove the statement to be true. In order to issue the just-quoted pronouncement with such confidence, Hitchens already has to have subscribed to the creed of a faith community for which scientism and scientific naturalism provide the dogmatic substance. And Hitchens must know that most people do not subscribe to that creed, perhaps because there is no "evidence" for it.

"Our god is *logos*," Freud proudly exclaims in *The Future of an Illusion,* candidly signifying the creedal character of the central dogma enshrined by the whole community of scientific rationalists.[2] The declaration makes for good class discussion, but whenever I asked my classes to evaluate Freud's claim that science is the only reliable road to truth, it did not take them long to recognize that the claim itself is logically self-defeating since it could never be justified by any conceivable scientific experiment. Most of my students would have had no difficulty realizing that scientism is also the self-subverting creed that provides the spongy cognitive foundation of the entire project we are dignifying with the label "new atheism."

Had they been required to read Harris's two books, my first-year collegiates would also hardly have failed to notice how often the Stanford graduate student exhorts his readers to give up their belief in God because it is not based on "evidence." Evidence is a word that shows up with great frequency in Harris's manifestoes, signifying its importance to the young scholar. But since it is clear that for Harris evidence really means what is available to scientific knowing, there is nothing in his working assumption that my students would not have encountered already in the empiricist naturalism that Freud and Russell adopt as their shared worldview.

For this reason, after taking "The Problem of God" course, the vast majority of our undergraduates would have deemed it silly for anyone to maintain that science can decide the question of God. Yet this is exactly what Richard Dawkins, the world's best-known evolutionist, claims in *The God Delusion* (48, 58–66). Harris and Hitchens also agree with Dawkins's assertion, even though they seem too circumspect to blurt it out so plainly. Science, Dawkins believes, can decide the question of God because of its potential command of all the relevant evidence. Yet this claim likewise makes no sense for the simple reason that scientific method by definition has nothing to say about God, meaning, values, or purpose. It took a long time for human thought to arrive at the point of realizing, in the sixteenth and seventeenth centuries, that it does not need to talk about God all the time when explaining how things work. So thinkers of great genius came up with a method of inquiry we now call "science," which can tell us a lot about the world by looking only at natural causes. But here we have Dawkins, who holds the Charles Simonyi Chair for the Public Understanding of Science at Oxford University, telling us that the question of God has now become appropriate subject matter for science too. Dawkins surely must notice the irony, but it does not bother him. "It may be," he confesses, "that humanity will never reach the quietus of complete understanding, but if we do, I venture the confident prediction that it will be science, not religion, that brings us there. And if that sounds like scientism, so much the better for scientism."[3] Being so explicit is an improvement on trying to cover up the new atheism's grounding assumption, but it does nothing to firm up the logical softness of that uncertain foundation.

Logic, however, was not the only issue that our introductory theology course had to consider. Also at stake was whether, if we seriously held atheism to be true, it would make a big difference to our lives and self-understanding. The new atheists, of course, would respond that it should make a big difference. But would it? We saw in the previous chapter how their four evident truths have the purpose of eliminating unnecessary misery and thus promoting happiness. But their popular and readable books offer no profound discussion of what "happiness" means.[4] The image of human fulfillment that emerges from their writings is one in which our present lifestyles will remain pretty much the same, minus the inconvenience of terrorism and creationists. Our new self-understanding will be informed by Darwinian biology, but we can expect that our moral and social instincts, rooted in biology as they are, will remain unmodified except for slight cultural corrections that will need to be made after religion disappears.

Unlike the sheltered circumstances that the socially conservative new atheism seeks to save, the classical atheists, whose writings my students were required to read, generally demanded a much more radical transformation of human culture and consciousness. This *transformation* became most evident when we moved on from Freud, Feuerbach, and Marx to the much more severe godlessness in works by Friedrich Nietzsche, Albert Camus, and Jean-Paul Sartre—the really hard-core atheists. To them atheism, if one is really serious about it, should make all the difference in the world, and it would take a superhuman effort to embrace it. "Atheism," as Sartre remarked, "is a cruel and long-range affair."[5] Along with Nietzsche and Camus, Sartre realized that most people will be too weak to accept the terrifying consequences of the death of God. However, anything less would be escapism, cowardice, and bad faith.

By contrast, my students would have noticed immediately that the authors I am examining in this book want atheism to prevail at the least possible expense to the agreeable socioeconomic circumstances out of which they sermonize. The new atheists' interest is in preserving rather than radically reforming the cultural milieu uncritically reflected in their wishes for a safer world. They would have the God religions—Judaism, Christianity, and Islam—simply disappear, after which we should be able go on enjoying the same lifestyle as before, only without the nuisance of suicide bombers and TV evangelists. We should be able to salvage the best that life has to offer right now, but without worrying about getting blown up by God-inspired fanatics.

Not that the new atheism, once implemented, would make no difference at all. But it would be a cosmetic correction in comparison with the seismic redefinition of human existence that the truly serious atheists demand. The two most significant changes the new atheists want to make are, first, that science rather than faith would become the foundation of the new world culture, as Freud and Russell had already anticipated; and, second, that morality would be rooted completely in reason. Science, they hope, would be emancipated from superstition, and the ethical instincts that natural selection has been sculpting in our species for over 2 million years would be finally liberated from their crippling bondage to religion.[6] People would then continue to cultivate essentially the same values as before, including altruism, but they would get along quite well without inspired books and divine commandments. Educators would be able to teach science without creationist intrusion, and students would learn that evolution rather than divine creativity is the ultimate explanation of why we are the kind of organisms we are. Only propositions based on "evidence" would be tolerated, but the satisfaction of knowing the truth about nature by way of science would compensate for any ethical constraints we would still have to put on our animal instincts.

This approach to atheism, of course, is precisely the kind that nauseated Nietzsche and made Camus and Sartre cringe in their Left Bank cafés. Atheism at the least possible expense to the mediocrity of Western culture is not atheism at all. It is nothing more than the persistence of life-numbing religiosity in a new guise. Please note that I am not promoting Camus's absurdist philosophy or Nietzschean and Sartrean nihilism either. But these more muscular critics of religion were at least smart enough to realize that a full acceptance of the death of God would require an asceticism completely missing in the new atheistic formulas. Atheism, as my students' acquaintance with Nietzsche, Camus, and Sartre would have clarified, must be thought out to its final logical conclusions. In this respect the new atheism, when measured against the stringent demands of a truly thoroughgoing unbelief, would be exposed as differing only superficially from the traditional theism it wants to replace. The blandness of the new soft-core atheism lies ironically in its willingness to compromise with the politically and culturally insipid kind of theism it claims to be ousting. Such a pale brand of atheism uncritically permits the same old values and meanings to hang around, only now they can become sanctified by an ethically and politically conservative Darwinian orthodoxy. If the new atheists' wishes are ever fulfilled, we need anticipate little in the way of cultural reform aside from turning the world's places of worship into museums, discos, and coffee shops.

In this respect the new atheism is very much like the old secular humanism rebuked by the hard-core atheists for its mousiness in facing up to what the absence of God should really mean. If you're going to be an atheist, the most rugged version of godlessness demands complete consistency. Go all the way and think the business of atheism through to the bitter end; before you get too comfortable with the godless world you long for, you will be required by the logic of any consistent skepticism to pass through the disorienting wilderness of nihilism. Do you have the courage to do that? You will have to adopt the tragic heroism of a Sisyphus, or realize that true freedom in the absence of God means that *you* are the creator of the values you live by, an intolerable burden from which most people would seek an escape. Are you ready to allow simple logic to lead you to the real truth about the death of God? Before settling into a truly atheistic worldview, you would have to experience the Nietzschean Madman's sensation of straying through "infinite nothingness." You would be required to summon up an unprecedented degree of courage if you plan to wipe away the whole horizon of transcendence. Are you willing to risk madness? If not, then you are not really an atheist.[7]

Predictably, nothing so shaking shows up in the thoughts of Dawkins, Harris, and Hitchens. Apart from the intolerance of tolerance, which we noted earlier, and the heavy dose of Darwinism that grounds many of its declarations, soft-core atheism differs scarcely at all from the older secular humanism that the hard-core atheists roundly chastised for its laxity. The new soft-core atheists assume that, by dint of Darwinism, we can just drop God like Santa Claus without having to witness the complete collapse of Western culture—including our sense of what is rational and moral. At least the hard-core atheists understood that if we are truly sincere in our atheism the whole web of meanings and values that had clustered around the idea of God in Western culture has to go down the drain along with its organizing center. Nietzsche, Camus, and Sartre, and perhaps several of their postmodern descendants, would have nothing to do with the vapid skepticism that fails to think atheism through with perfect consistency.

"If anyone has written a book more critical of religious faith than I have, I'm not aware of it," declares Sam Harris.[8] My students might not be so sure. Has Harris really thought about what would happen if people adopted the hard-core atheist's belief that there is no transcendent basis for our moral valuations? What if people had the sense to ask whether Darwinian naturalism can provide a solid and enduring foundation for our truth claims and value judgments? Would a good science education make everyone simply decide to be good if the universe is inherently valueless and purposeless? At least the hard-core atheists tried to prepare their readers for the pointless world they would encounter if the death of God were ever taken seriously. They did not form a project to kill God since they assumed that deicide had already taken place at the hands of scientism and secularism. But they wanted people to face up *honestly* to the logical, ethical, and cultural implications of a godless world.

Nietzsche, Camus, and Sartre also failed to embody the tragic heroism that they thought should be the logical outcome of atheism. They turned out to be very much like the rest of us. Still, their failure actually fortifies the conclusion that at least some of my students arrived at in "The Problem of God" course: a truly consistent atheism is impossible to execute. And if hard-core atheism cannot succeed, it is doubtful that the soft-core variety will make it either. After reading Nietzsche's fevered discourses about the creation of new values that would need to take place once people realize that the God idea is fiction, the actual ethical prescriptions he endorsed ended up sounding at best like a juiced up version of the old. He thought that once we realize there is no Creator, our own newly liberated creativity would be able to impregnate with wholly new meanings and values the infinite emptiness left behind. After we have drunk up the sea of transcendence, there should be endless room for a whole new set of ethical imperatives. Yet one can only be disappointed with what Nietzsche devised. His new set of rules for life sound at one extreme suspiciously like monkish asceticism, and at the other like run-of-the-mill secular humanism: "Be creative." "Don't live lives of mediocrity!" "Don't listen to those who speak of otherworldly hopes!" "Remain faithful to the earth." Nietzsche in no way leaves behind what he first heard from the Bible. His call to a fresh "innocence of becoming" and "newness of life" is at least a faint echo of the biblical prophets and Paul, only without the virtues of love and hope.[9]

Similarly, Camus made a curious transition—without telling us exactly why—from the absurdism of his early writings, *The Stranger* and *The Myth of Sisyphus*, to the moving humanism of *The Plague* and the rather traditionalist preoccupation with moral guilt in *The Fall*. He must have come to realize that the utter hopelessness of his early nihilistic atheism could not provide a space within which people can actually live their lives. Meanwhile Sartre, once he had assured us that there are no God-given commandments, ended up sounding almost religious in issuing his "new" imperative, namely, "Accept your freedom!" For the early Sartre it was always wrong ("bad faith") to deny our freedom and that of others. But as much as he wanted all of this to sound radically new, in order to make his atheism palatable he had to argue that his "existentialism" is really a form of "humanism" after all.[10] So if even the hard-core atheists fail to carry out their program of erasing every trace of transcendent values from their moral universe, then how much less can our soft-core atheists expect, logically speaking, to accomplish such a goal?[11]

## RIGHTNESS

The hard-core atheists set very exacting standards about who will be allowed into the society of genuine unbelief. They insisted that every serious atheist must think out fully what atheism logically entails, even if they did not succeed in doing so themselves. The new soft-core atheists don't even try. They agree with their hard-core cousins that God does not exist. But where logical rigor would require that they also acknowledge that there is no timeless heaven to determine what is good and what is not, their ideas go limp instead. Our new atheists remain as committed unconditionally to traditional values as the rest of us. They do so most openly in every claim they make that religious faith is bad, and that for the sake of true values moral people must rid themselves of it as soon as they can!

All three of our soft-core atheists are absolutely certain that the creeds, ideals, and practices of religion are essentially evil. In fact, a distinguishing mark of the new atheism is that it leaves no room for a sense of moral ambiguity in anything that smacks of faith. There is no allowance that religion might have at least one or two redeeming features. No such waffling is permitted. Their hatred of religious faith is so palpable that the pages of their books fairly quiver in our hands. Such outrage, however, can arise only from a sense of being deeply grounded in an unmovable realm of "rightness." The fervor in the new atheists' outrage against faith, and especially belief in God, is as resolute as any evangelist could marshal. To know with such certitude that religion is evil, one must first have already surrendered one's heart and mind to what is unconditionally good. But in making this surrender our critics must not be very far from exemplifying the theological understanding of faith that I sketched at the end of chapter 1.

The books by Dawkins, Harris, and Hitchens are not mild treatises like those that trickle tentatively, and often unreadably, from departments of philosophy. They are works of passion, and I suspect that most philosophers would be embarrassed by their intemperate style of presentation. So I do not expect that philosophers will recommend these writings to their own students either, although the books might usefully serve as case studies for classes in critical thinking. At their most tender point, that of justifying the values that lie behind their moral evaluation of religion, logical coherence abandons each of the new atheists.

With the hard-core atheists one has to ask this newer breed: What is the basis of your moral rectitude? How, in other words, if there is no eternal ground of values, can your own strict standards be anything other than arbitrary, conventional, historically limited human concoctions? But you take them as absolutely binding. And if you are a Darwinian, how can your moral values ultimately be anything more than blind contrivances of evolutionary selection? But, again, in your condemnation of the evils of religion, you must be assuming a standard of goodness so timeless and absolute as to be God-given. Of course, no one objects to your making moral judgments. But if you, your tribe, or mindless Mother Nature are the ultimate ground of your values, why does your sense of rightness function with such assuredness in your moral indictment of all people of faith? Can your own frail lives and easily impressionable minds—since you are human just like the rest of us—be the source of something so adamantine as your own sense of rightness? "Excuse us for being so direct," my students would ask, "but if you are going to fall back now on evolutionary biology, how can random events and blind natural selection account for the *absoluteness* that you in fact attribute to the values that justify your intolerance of faith? Or, if you do not want Darwin to give the whole answer, can the historically varying winds of human culture account fully for the rocklike solidity of your righteousness?"

Dawkins declares that the biblical God is a monster; Harris, that God is evil; Hitchens, that God is not great. But without some fixed sense of rightness, how can one distinguish what is monstrous, evil, or "not great" from its opposite? In order to make such value judgments, one must assume, as the hard-core atheists are honest enough to acknowledge, that there exists somewhere, in some mode of being, a realm of rightness that does not owe its existence completely to human invention, Darwinian selection, or social construction. If we allow the hard-core atheists into our discussion we can draw this conclusion: If absolute values exist, then God exists. But if God does not exist, then neither do absolute values, and one should not issue moral judgments as if they do.

Belief in God or the practice of religion, as I shall emphasize later, is not necessary in order for people to be highly moral beings. We can agree with our soft-core atheists on this point. But the real question, which comes not from me but from the hard-core atheists, is: Can you rationally justify your unconditional adherence to timeless values without implicitly invoking the existence of God? The hard-core atheists say "no." We return to this question in chapter 6.

# 3
# *Does Theology Matter?*

Science has become the preeminent sphere for the demonstration of intellectual honesty. Pretending to know things you do not know is a great liability in science; and yet, it is the *sine qua non* of faith-based religion.

—Sam Harris[1]

The new atheists unveil religion at its absolute ugliest. They are not interested in taking a balanced approach essential to real scholarship. Serving up the most extreme forms of rabid religiosity, they try to convince their readers that this repugnant material is the essence of faith. What most of us consider the most objectionable religious expressions sum up for the new atheists what the theistic faiths are really all about. Like their religious opponents, the new atheists are just as closed off to open-ended dialogue with theologians as are anti-Darwinians such as Henry Morris, Ken Ham, and Duane Gish. Harris complains that "there is just no talking to some people," but after reading his two books and those of Dawkins and Hitchens, it is hard to imagine how an open-minded theological conversation with any of these uncompromising critics could ever get off the ground either.

Unfortunately, the new atheists do not care at all whether theologians read their books. In fact, they would prefer not. They are not writing for theologians but for the masses of theologically uninformed readers. Anyway, in their view theology is just a tedious, nit-picking defense of the emptiness and idiocies of religious faith. Why waste time actually reading theology, let alone studying or taking a course in it? Having been trained to recognize what constitutes appropriate "evidence," the three critics find it incredible that anyone would pay attention to theology at all.

In each of the books under review, theologians come in for the most venomous sarcasm of all. "Surely there must come a time," Harris remarks, "when we will acknowledge the obvious: theology is now little more than a branch of human ignorance. Indeed, it is ignorance with wings" (173). Dawkins, for his part, thinks he has gained sufficient expertise to dismiss all of theology simply by virtue of his being schooled in science. Questions about whether Mary was a virgin, whether Jesus rose from the dead, and even whether God exists are for him strictly scientific questions and deserve strictly scientific answers (58–59). The methods a good theologian should use "in the unlikely event that relevant evidence ever became available, would be purely and entirely scientific methods" (59).

## LITERALISM

In preparing treatises on *a*-theism, one would expect that scholars and journalists would have done some research on *theism*, just to be sure they know exactly what they are rejecting. It is hard to be an informed and consistent atheist without knowing something about theology, but aside from several barbed references there is no sign of any contact between the new atheists and theology, let alone studious investigation of the topic. This circumvention is comparable to creationists rejecting evolution without ever having taken a course in biology. They just *know* there's something wrong with those crazy Darwinian fantasies, just as the new atheists just *know* there is something sick and delusional about theology. There is no need to look at it up close. Furthermore, conversation with theologians, most of whom are not biblical literalists, would add a dimension of intricacy to the new atheist literature that would detract from the breeziness that sells books.

Ignorance of theology simplifies the new atheists' attacks on their equally uninformed religious adversaries. It allows their critique to match, point for point, the fundamentalism it is trying to eliminate. In fact, on the wide spectrum of contemporary atheism Dawkins, Harris, and Hitchens epitomize the scientifically literalist extreme almost in the same way that the religious fundamentalists they condemn represent the literalist extreme in the wide world of Jewish, Christian, and Islamic thought. The resemblance is not coincidental. Both scientific and religious literalists share the belief that there is nothing beneath the surface of the texts they are reading—nature in the case of science, sacred Scriptures in the case of religion. Scientism, the scientific community's version of literalism, assumes that the universe becomes fully transparent only if it is packaged in the impersonal language of mathematics or other kinds of scientific modeling. Any intuition that a deeper drama might be going on beneath the surface of nature, as religion and theology maintain, is pure fiction. Similarly, the religious literalist assumes that the full depth of what is going on in the real world is made evident to the true believer in the plainest sense of the sacred texts. So there is no reason to look beneath the literal sense, or raise new questions about the meaning of these texts when circumstances change dramatically from one age to the next. Both sides steer clear of theology.

In order to give uninformed readers the impression that he has done at least some theological research, Richard Dawkins drops the names of several reputable contemporary theologians and even provides a few brief quotes (147–50). But these insignificant morsels are not enough to cover up the more typically creationist and historically anachronistic mentality that he brings to his reading of the Bible and theology as well. His own implicit version of theological method is exactly the same as that of "scientific creationists," notorious in theological circles for their belief that, if the Bible is inspired by God, it must be a reliable source of scientific as well as spiritual information. The only significant difference that I can see between Dawkins and his creationist antagonists is that Dawkins considers the Bible and theology to be unreliable sources of scientific information, whereas the creationists do not. His uncompromising literalism is nowhere more obvious than in his astonishing insistence throughout *The God Delusion* that the notion of God should be treated as a scientific hypothesis, subject to the same verificational procedures as any other "scientific" hypothesis. He has no doubt that the hypothesis will not hold up under investigation, but determining whether it will or not is not a theological but "a scientific question" (48). I have more to say about Dawkins and the God hypothesis in the next chapter.

In considering the Bible, Hitchens also shares with his extremist religious adversaries the assumption that grasping the full substance of biblical faith requires that the sacred texts be taken literally. Why else, for example, would he argue seriously that because of the evangelists' contradictions on dates, the details of Jesus' crucifixion, and other topics, the four Gospels cannot all claim "divine warrant" (112). He seems unaware that exegetes and theologians have known about these discrepancies since antiquity, but they have not been so literalist as to interpret insignificant factual contradictions as threats to the doctrine of biblical inspiration. Particularly puzzling to Hitchens are the infancy narratives in the Gospels of Matthew and Luke. Most Christian scholars today delight in these factually irreconcilable accounts of Jesus' birth, since through them the two evangelists are able to introduce idiosyncratic theological themes that they carry through the remainder of their Gospels. Hitchens, however, cannot get over how anybody could possibly take them seriously as the Word of God if they are so factually divergent (111–12). So he concludes: "Either the gospels are in some sense literal truth, or the whole thing is essentially a fraud and perhaps an immoral one at that" (120). As if this were not enough to make educated readers wince, any prospect that Hitchens is trying to impress scholars completely vanishes when he says in passing that Jesus' very existence is "highly questionable" (114). Hitchens also reveals to us that theism's "foundational books are transparent fables," and that, in light of today's scientific understanding of the origin of the cosmos and the origin of species, those foundational books (presumably Genesis in particular) and the religion they inspire are consigned to "marginality if not irrelevance" (229)!

Few theologians today would take Hitchens's method of measuring the Bible's worth in terms of its scientific credibility any more seriously than they do the scientific creationism from which Hitchens seems to have picked up his own exegetical style. Students who take an introductory course in biblical literature learn to take all these contradictions in stride, seeing them as opportunities to explore deeper levels of the sacred texts or as invitations to study the diverse theological perspectives in the Bible. By the time they have finished a good undergraduate course in biblical literature, most Christian and Jewish students will have overcome their initial puzzlement at the historical inaccuracies, the sinfulness of characters in the Bible, and the crudity of some of its images of God. They would have outgrown the naive idea that biblical inspiration means divine dictation—something that Harris has not yet discovered. Students would have become reconciled to the idea that revelation has nothing to do with the communication of scientific information and that therefore a biblical theology of origins does not contradict Darwinian science. Meanwhile, Hitchens remains outside the classroom door grousing about the non-Mosaic authorship of the Pentateuch (104). And Harris is still wondering how a book allegedly "written by God" (35) or "authored by the Creator of the universe" turns out to be "the work of sand-strewn men and women who thought the earth was flat . . ." (45).

So the important difference between the new atheist and the creationist is not that one side claims to take science seriously and the other does not. They both at least profess to do so. Nor is it that one side expects the Bible to provide scientific information and the other does not. They both assume that allegedly inspired literature should do at least that much. Rather, the significant difference is that the creationist considers the Bible a *reliable* source of science whereas the new atheist does not. But the important point to keep in mind is that the new atheist places the same literalist demands on the Bible as do Christian and other fundamentalists.

This literalism is disappointing to those who wish to avoid confusing religion with science. But none of our critics will permit any such clear distinction, and in this respect as well they dwell comfortably within the company of creationists. Harris, for example, insists that "the same evidentiary demands"—that is, the same scientific standards—must be used to measure the truth status of religious propositions as any others. He wonders why all benighted Bible readers are not as befuddled as he is that "a book written by an omniscient being" would fail to be "the richest source of mathematical insight humanity has ever known," or why the Bible has nothing to say "about electricity, or about DNA, or about the actual age and size of the universe" (*Letter to a Christian Nation*, 60–61). In thirty-five years of undergraduate teaching I never encountered a single instance where, at least after taking a theology course, a student would be capable of making such a farcical complaint. But Harris, like the creationists he denounces, and unlike theologically informed students, wants nothing to do with an allegedly inspired text that fails to give useful and accurate scientific information.

In 1893, even the very conservative Pope Leo XIII, in his encyclical *Providentissimus Deus,* instructed Catholics never to look for scientific information in the Bible. On this point Dawkins, Harris, and Hitchens take their stand far to the right of Pope Leo. They might easily have avoided this bungle had they but gone back several centuries and taken heed of Galileo. In the seventeenth century this scientific giant and devout Catholic, in his brilliant "Letter to the Grand Duchess Christina," pointed out that the biblical authors could not possibly have intended to deliver scientifically accurate propositions about the natural world. If that had been their intention, the least little slipup in their science would also have made intelligent readers suspicious of their religious message as well. "Hence," Galileo comments, "I should think it would be the part of prudence not to permit anyone to usurp scriptural texts and force them in some way to maintain any physical conclusions to be true, when at some future time the senses and demonstrative or necessary reasons may show the contrary."[2] Yet even today scientific naturalists no less than biblical literalists still interpret religious doctrines and Scriptures as though their intention is to solve scientific puzzles. Much earlier than Galileo, Augustine's *De Genesi ad literam* had advised readers of Genesis not to get hung up on questions about its astronomical exactness, nor try to defend the literal accuracy of its cosmological assumptions. Otherwise unbelievers are likely to dismiss the biblical writings "when they teach, relate, and deliver more profitable matters."[3]

Of course, for the new atheists there simply cannot be any more "profitable matters." If biblical truth cannot be reduced to scientific truth, then it does not qualify as truth in any sense. And it should be known that Dawkins, Harris, and Hitchens are not alone among new atheists who chastise the biblical authors for not getting their science right. For example, the philosopher Daniel Dennett, reading the Bible at the same literalist level as creationists, remarks that evolutionary biology is incompatible with biblical belief. Contrasting the sorry state of scientific information in the Bible to that of present-day biology, he tries to shock us into confessing with him that "science has won and religion has lost," and that "Darwin's idea has banished the Book of Genesis to the limbo of quaint mythology."[4] Here again it is only because he embraces a creationist hermeneutical method that Dennett can claim so triumphantly that evolutionary biology has exposed Genesis as a mere fossil.

If theologians were cooperative enough to deal in the currency of scientific "evidence" and information, the new atheists suggest, then theology might be worth a second look. As it is, however, big bang cosmology and the biological sciences are enough to convince Dennett, Hitchens, Harris, and Dawkins that theological tracts on such topics as divine creation or God's authorship of life are now obsolete. Since ancient texts and modern theological interpretations fail to improve our scientific understanding, we can safely ignore them. For the new atheist, therefore, apparently it is scientific questions that can unlock the deepest content of classic religious texts. Yet one of the first lessons college theology students learn is that if they fail to ask the right questions of any classic text, religious or otherwise, they will miss its meaning altogether. This is a basic principle of textual interpretation in general, and of theological method in particular. To read Homer only for the purpose of learning about ancient culinary habits may be informative, but that kind of questioning will not lead us to learn any lessons about life that *The Iliad* and *The Odyssey* may have to teach us. Any deeper wisdom in these great works would pass us by.

Likewise, asking the Qur'an or the Bible to inform us about things we can find out for ourselves by reason or science alone can only distract us from any possible deeper illumination they may have to offer. The business of theology is to make sure that our questions to the Scriptures of any religious tradition will be directed in such a way as to allow ourselves to be challenged and even shaken at the deepest levels of our existence by what the text has to say. But one way to prevent any such encounter is to approach the texts, as do the new atheists, armed with nothing but scientific curiosity or, as we shall see later, simplistic questions about morality. The accounts of origins in the Bible have the purpose of awakening gratitude, humility, confidence, and hope in the communities for whom they were composed. Creationists are wrong to read the creation stories as science, but at least they can pick up some of the religious challenge of the texts in spite of their anachronistic exegesis. But the new atheists cannot even do this much. They share the untimely scientific reading with creationists, but being also deaf to the clearly transformative intent of the Scriptures, they completely disqualify themselves as interpreters of biblical faith.

The new atheists, none of whom exhibits scholarly expertise in the field of religious studies, have methodically avoided theologians and biblical scholars as irrelevant to the kind of instruction their books are intended to provide. Instead, they have acquired their expertise in religious studies by limiting their research almost exclusively to the doctrinaire radicals and reactionaries about whom they are warning us. In order to grasp what religion really is, the atheists imply, all we need to focus on are its extremists, literalist interpreters, super-sectarians, inquisitors, and terrorists. I am surprised that they left out the history of the papacy, wherein one can find some of the most indecorous instances of religious degradation. Our self-taught experts in religion, in contrast to the thousands of academic scholars and literate ministers they ignore, are saying to their readers that the only features of faith worth talking about are those to which fundamentalists and fanatics have turned our attention.

This does not mean that the books we are reviewing have no valid points to make about the many abuses sponsored by religions and theologies. Of course they do, and most readers will find themselves agreeing with the negative judgments on the barbarities that have accompanied human religiosity from the start. For this reason the cataloging of the evils of religion and theology in these bestsellers may be instructive to nonscholars. But readers have every right to expect balance and fairness from journalists and academics. They do not receive that from Hitchens, Dawkins, and Harris. In a sense, this is not surprising since the authors bring no scholarly expertise to their diatribes, and everyone knows that ignorance about what one is rejecting always leads to caricature.

Consequently, since fairness is not important, our critics rely mostly on rhetorical trickery, a very unscholarly way to convince people, but one that mimics in every way the demonizing mind-set of the various fundamentalisms they loathe. Very seldom, if ever, do they invite readers to inspect anything but the seamiest side of religious life. In fact, all three authors go through contortions to convince readers that no other side exists. This is nowhere more painful to watch than in Hitchens's awkward attempt to disassociate the message of Martin Luther King Jr. from that of the prophets and Jesus. If one really believes that "religion poisons everything," then King's message, which Hitchens admires, must be disentangled from the Bible as well as the vile history of religion and theology.

Theologians, meanwhile, have known about the evils of religion much longer and in much more sordid detail and depth than our ill-informed new atheists. They have also presented much more impressive critiques of religion than have the latter.[5] Not to be outdone, however, the new atheists deem it necessary to say a few nasty things about the discipline of theology (or what they call a "non-subject") and then throw it away with everything else religious. To discredit it completely, Dawkins, Hitchens, and especially Harris first have to convince their readers that theology is a most blameworthy accomplice of religious atrocity. How so? Simply by making room for faith and belief in God, theology has created the cultural and cognitive space in which religious abuse can occur. The most efficient way to rid the world of religious fanaticism is thus to close up any plausible opening for religious faith in the first place. Ridding the world of theology would be a major step on the road to a world without fanatics. Such a program is comparable, of course, to abolishing sex abuse by first abolishing sex.

The main reason for Harris's contempt for theology is that theologians have been the most irresponsible promoters of what he calls the liberal tolerance of faith. A good example, one that the new atheists leave out as far as I can tell, is the Second Vatican Council's document on religious liberty. The theology that went into shaping that document, they would point out, promotes the sort of tolerance of faith that gives rise to so much of the world's recent religious violence. Simply by accepting the rights of people to subscribe without penalty to the religion of their choice, and therefore to have a "faith," theology has granted extremists the opportunity to kill people in the name of their gods. The council's statement, therefore, should be considered just one more expression of the liberal theology that is to blame for the persistence of religious immoderation anywhere.

The new atheists scarcely notice the irony in their intolerance of religious tolerance. On the one hand they bring up past inquisitions as evidence of the evils of religion, but on the other they now excoriate theological moderates who espouse the new spirit of tolerance. Moreover, they seem not to notice that the very same liberal tolerance in modern Western history that influenced the Catholic Church to change its stand on religious freedom provides the cultural space and freedom of expression by which the new atheists themselves are permitted to vent their own literalist ideas. Even the vaguest knowledge of humanity's sorrowful struggle toward tolerance and religious freedom would make most people hesitate before promoting the intolerance of tolerance.

* * *

Science, the new atheists claim, now proves that theology no longer matters at all. And yet their own cult of science parallels the most inflexible versions of theology in making the world smaller than it really is. Scientism is to science what literalism is to faith. It is a way of shrinking the world so as to make it manageable and manipulable. It is a way of suppressing the anxiety that might arise from a more open, courageous, and wholesome encounter with mystery. Scientism's main motive is fear of losing control. We can observe the narrowing instinct at work in the religious literalism that reads sacred texts as though their purpose is to provide scientific information or lists of sexual acts to be avoided. And we can also see it at work in the cascade of shrinkages that the new atheists have to push through in order to take religion out of the hands of theology and put it in the steadier hands of scientists where they think it really belongs. The shrinkages include:

- Reducing, or trying hard to reduce, the entire monotheistic religious population to scriptural literalists, dogmatic extremists, escapists, perverts, perpetrators of human suffering, and fanatics.
- Reducing the cultural role of theology to the systematic underwriting of religious abuse.
- Reducing the meaning of faith to mindless belief in whatever has no evidence.
- Reducing the meaning of "evidence" to "what is available to science."
- Reducing the whole of reality to what can be known by science.

- Reducing the idea of God to a "hypothesis" (Dawkins 31–73).

Of course, like their opponents, the new atheists are so confident that they are in complete possession of the truth that they consider it pointless to expose their own beliefs to open dialogue. When it comes to the topic of religion, the new atheists mirror their extremist opponents in assuming that they are in complete and inalterable possession of the truth. As distinct from those who allow themselves to be gradually transformed by a dialogical encounter with the views of others, extremists fear that open conversation will lead at best to a softening of the hard mound of certainty on which they believe they stand. Nevertheless, in the case of the new atheists the pulpit may not be perched as firmly on pure reason and openness to truth as they suppose. The following chapters provide further grounds for this suspicion.

# 4

# *Is God a Hypothesis?*

The atheist, by merely being in touch with reality, appears
shamefully out of touch with the fantasy life of his neighbors.
—Sam Harris[1]

Just those who feel they are . . . most fully objective in their
assessment of reality, are most in the power of deep unconscious fantasies.
—Robert Bellah[2]

Being an atheist is not always easy, especially in the United
States. There can be no doubt that atheists are unjustly discrim-
inated against, and every instance of hatred directed toward
them by Christians, Jews, or Muslims only drives them deeper
into their own circle of certainty. In the company of fellow unbelievers they find mutual encouragement to continue the good
fight. The assembly is still relatively spare, but it is ample and
secure enough these days to provide relief from the feeling of
estrangement felt by many atheists in the past. The need for fel-
lowship is as powerful among unbelievers as believers, and Web
sites, blogs, books, journals, and conferences provide a growing
network of support for atheists. The new atheists still exaggerate
their cultural influence, but the enthusiastic popular reception of
their books reveals a significant sector of doubters who normally
keep their skepticism under wraps. All in all, the comfort zone
for antitheism seems to be warming up gradually. In the academic world the popularity of scientific naturalism provides a
cozy intellectual habitat for the new atheists and other skeptics.

Scientific naturalism, the main tenets of which I listed in the
Introduction, is now a major worldview among intellectuals.

Owen Flanagan, a philosopher at Duke University, even goes so far as to say that the ideal vocation of academic philosophers today is to make the world safe for "naturalism," by which he means atheism.[3] In my own work I have met numerous academic philosophers, as well as other scholars, who embrace Flanagan's ideal. In almost all such cases the intellectual basis for their atheism is scientific naturalism's claim that science alone can be trusted to put our minds in touch with reality. What this means for our soft-core atheists is that if there is no scientifically accessible evidence to support belief in God, then by default atheism must be true. Surely they have heard the maxim that absence of evidence for God is not evidence of absence, but, if they have, they ignore it. In addition to lack of "evidence," the new atheists generally insist that there are also moral grounds for rejecting belief in God. These moral reasons, expressed in their outrage at the wickedness of religions throughout the ages, are probably the most striking aspect of their atheism, but I save the discussion of morality and faith until chapters 6 and 8. At present I want to focus only on the question of "evidence."

## THE GOD HYPOTHESIS

The argumentative strategy of the new atheists is, first, to seduce readers into tacit agreement that faith in the existence of God is a "hypothesis," one that functions for believers in the same way as a scientific hypothesis does for scientists (Dawkins 31–73).[4] In science, a hypothesis is a conceptual framework for bringing intelligibility to a range of repeatable observations or experiments. But is God a hypothesis? It has not escaped Dawkins's attention that intelligent design (ID) proponents resort to something like a God hypothesis to explain biological complexity. ID advocates, all of whom are theists, think of intelligent design as functioning like a *scientific* hypothesis—or more precisely, a scientific theory—standing in opposition to evolutionary theory. Although not all ID proponents explicitly identify the intelligent designer as God, it is clear that they are resorting to a supernatural agency as though it were a scientific explanation. Not surprisingly, Dawkins seizes this theological impropriety as warrant for his own assumption that the idea of God functions, or should function, for all theists as a rival scientific hypothesis to that of evolutionary biology. For Dawkins, being a supernatural designer is essential to the very definition of God (31), and so he is eager to go along with ID in placing God in the role of a hypothesis.

The fact is that the idea of God functions as anything but a scientific hypothesis for most believers and theologians, but this does not deter Dawkins and his associates. Indeed, a key component of the new atheists' case against God is to suppose that creationism and ID represent the intellectual high point and central core of theistic traditions. Most contemporary theologians reject creationism and ID for theological reasons, but the new atheists have decided, almost by decree, that theology does not count and should be kept out of their discussions about God. Having avoided any substantive encounter with theology, the second part of the new atheists' argument is simple: pointing out that there is no evidence to support the God hypothesis.

A constant refrain of the new atheists is as follows: the fundamental problem with faith is that it is based on no "evidence," or at best on insufficient evidence, and therefore must be rejected in all its forms. Science by contrast can point to countless reproducible observations that support its own hypotheses, and whereas a good scientist is willing to give up or modify a hypothesis if the experiments require doing so, the faithful cling to their God hypothesis no matter how nonexistent the evidence. Finally, as Hitchens takes great pleasure in reminding us (68–71), science has shown the God hypothesis to be a violation of Occam's razor. Occam's razor is an axiom of science that states in effect that we should never resort to a complex explanation when a simpler one will do. Consequently, if science can explain biological complexity in a simple way, then of what use is the (more complex) doctrine of divine creation? The God hypothesis is a pseudoscientific attempt to do what science can now do much better by itself. Thus, all reasonable people should reject the God hypothesis and embrace science as the surest way to orient their thoughts and lives. (I discuss Hitchens's, as well as Dawkins's, misuse of Occam's razor in chapter 7.)

Dawkins's two-pronged argumentative strategy is intended to deliver the decisive intellectual blow to theism, and hence establish atheism as "almost certain" (113–59). However, Dawkins and the other new atheists have made things entirely too easy for themselves. In the first place, as is typical of all their writings, in order to dispose of God they first shrink the idea of divinity to that of a lawgiver, cosmic engineer, or intelligent designer (Dawkins 31). This sets the stage for showing everybody that Darwinian evolution obviously proves that nature was not intelligently designed after all, and that the God hypothesis has at last been decisively defeated. So impressed are Dawkins and other evolutionary naturalists by this argument that they present themselves as the intellectual superiors of all believers. Sometimes these days they even refer to themselves as "brights," thereby distinguishing themselves from their not-so-bright religious opponents.[5] Yet there is nothing terribly bright about debating creationism and ID while avoiding any direct engagement with theology. The new atheists make no mention, for example, of the most important Protestant theologian of the past century, Karl Barth, who, along with most other recent theologians, has argued in effect that any God who functions as a "hypothesis" is not worth defending anyway. The new atheists are actually doing theology a favor by disposing of the God hypothesis.

Why so? Because thinking of God as a hypothesis reduces the infinite divine mystery to a finite scientific cause, and to worship anything finite is idolatrous. The notion of a God hypothesis shrinks God down to the size of a link in a causal chain, and this diminishment amounts to a much more radical atheism than our three purveyors of godlessness could ever have concocted by themselves. The real work of atheism had already been accomplished in the early modern age by careless Christian thinkers who reduced God to a first efficient cause in a physical system.[6] So the new, soft-core atheists have arrived at the scene of God's murder far too late. On each new page of their manifestoes we find them pummeling a corpse.

Criticizing theistic faiths without taking into account the work of theologians such as Karl Barth or Paul Tillich (and many others) is like trying to explain the natural world while leaving out any mention of modern science. In their critiques of the God hypothesis, the new atheists demonstrate that they have only the shallowest, if any, acquaintance with any major theologian or theological tradition. Nor do they suffer the slightest embarrassment at the fact that they have chosen to topple a deity whose existence most theologians and a very large number of other Christians, Muslims, and Jews would have no interest in defending anyway.

Dawkins would reply that he is refuting each and every understanding of God (36), but he clearly thinks of God in an extremely limited, indeed twisted, way when he defines "God" as a hypothetical supernatural designer. The snapshot of God that he flashes in *The God Delusion* is a caricature that has long been offensive to theology. It seems to come almost exclusively from visiting the campsites and Web sites of creationists and ID defenders. Moreover, by insisting that the God hypothesis is subject to being confirmed or falsified only by scientific method, Dawkins has set up a problem that has nothing whatsoever to do with either science or theology. Any deity whose existence could be decided by something as cheap as "evidence" in Harris's or Dawkins's vulgar understanding of that term could never command anyone's worship. So by avoiding theology altogether, the new atheism has once again shown itself to be irrelevant except to those who share its emaciated understanding of God.

## WHERE IS GOD?

If faith in God is truthful, then, as the new atheists rightly point out, there must be something in reality that corresponds to the idea of God. But, according to Dawkins, Harris, and Hitchens, no such correspondence can be shown empirically to exist. Since faith gives rise to all sorts of fantasies, how do we know that the idea of God is not just as wild and removed from reality as belief in the tooth fairy? As Harris insists, in order to be accepted as true there has to be a way of confirming the reality of God independently of faith (50–79). Given that science has not been able to find God, and the prospects that it will ever do so are not good, atheism is the only reasonable position left.

But if faith in God requires independent scientific confirmation, what about the colossal faith our new atheists place in science itself? Exactly what are the independent scientific experiments, we might ask, that could provide "evidence" for the hypothesis that all true knowledge must be based on the paradigm of scientific inquiry? If faith requires independent confirmation, what is the independent (nonfaith) method of demonstrating that their own faith in the all-encompassing cognitional scope of science is reasonable? If science itself is the only way to provide such independent assessment, then the quest for proper validation only moves the justification process in the direction of an infinite regress.

What's more, there are many channels other than science through which we all experience, understand, and know the world. In my interpersonal knowledge, for example, the evidence that someone loves me is hard to measure, but it can be very real nonetheless. The only way I can encounter the subjective depth of another person is to abandon the objectifying method of science. To treat the otherness and subjectivity of another person as though he or she were just another object in nature is both cognitively and morally wrong. To take account of the evidence of subjective depth that I encounter in the face of another person, I need to adopt a stance of vulnerability. Encounter with another's personal depth challenges me to put aside the controlling, mastering, objectifying method of natural science. Likewise, in my encounter with a work of great artistic value or with the beauty in nature, the aesthetic "evidence" is such that I will miss it completely unless I abandon the objectifying, analytical stance and allow myself to be carried away by it.

Do our new atheists seriously believe, therefore, that if a personal God of infinite beauty and unbounded love actually exists, the "evidence" for this God's existence could be gathered as cheaply as the evidence for a scientific hypothesis? Even in our ordinary human experience it is other personal subjects that matter most to us, and no amount of scientific expertise can tell us who they really are. Would it be otherwise with God, whom believers experience not as an ordinary "It" but as a supreme "Thou"? If God exists, then interpersonal experience, not the impersonal objectivity of science, would be essential to knowledge of this God. In our everyday existence the love of another person matters more to us than almost anything else, but gathering the "evidence" for that love requires a leap of trust on our part, a wager that renders us vulnerable to their special kind of presence. The other person's love, moreover, captures us in such a way that we cannot connect with it at all if we try to control it intellectually. Again, would it be otherwise in the case of any conceivable encounter of human persons with an infinite love?

Since God matters more than anything else to devout believers, how could they know God without risking themselves, or without undergoing a deep personal change analogous to, but more dramatic than, what it takes to know the love of another human being? All the great faith traditions insist that the encounter with ultimate reality cannot occur without such a transformation. The life of faith is one in which "there is no knowing without going":[7] "unless you change and become like children, you will never enter the kingdom of heaven" (Matt. 18:3). Even to understand the world in a scientific, objectifying way requires a very specific kind of training, asceticism, and mental transformation. So if the universe is encompassed by an infinite Love, would the encounter with this ultimate reality require anything less than a posture of receptivity and readiness to surrender to its embrace? How is it that the new atheists think they can decide the question of God's existence without having opened themselves to the personal transformation essential to faith's sense of being grasped by an unbounded love?

Clearly the new atheists are looking for a shortcut and a direct, objectifying access to what believers regard as unapproachable apart from the surrender of faith. Not finding God or any "evidence" of God by way of either scientific or ordinary ways of knowing, they are now certain that God does not exist.

## THE NEED FOR FAITH

At some point in the validation of every truth claim or hypothesis, a leap of faith is an inescapable ingredient. At the foundation of every human search for understanding and truth, including the scientific search, an ineradicable element of trust is present. If you find yourself doubting what I have just said, it is only because, at this very moment, you trust your own mind enough to express concern about my assertion. You cannot avoid trusting your intellectual capacity, even when you are in doubt. Moreover, you raise your critical questions only because you *believe* that truth is worth seeking. Faith in this sense, and *not* in the sense of wild imaginings and wishful thinking, lies at the root of all authentic religion—and science.

Trust is another word for what the Christian Scriptures call faith, and only a little reflection is needed to notice that every inquiry of every human being emerges from the murkiness of some sort of faith, or trust, without objective evidence. Most of us simply believe that seeking truth is worthwhile. We cannot prove it since even the attempt to do so already presupposes this trust. This basic trust, then, launches and energizes every honest human inquiry, not least the scientific search itself. But my point is that this basic trust is not the outcome of any regime of scientific experimentation. Trusting that the natural world is intelligible and that truth is worth seeking is essential to getting science off the ground in the first place. We spontaneously trust that our journeys of exploration will be greeted by an ever-expanding field of intelligibility and an inexhaustible depth of truth. This trust also lies at the heart of genuine religious faith. In this respect, at least, science and faith are allies, not enemies. A mysterious and irrepressible font of trust wells up from deep within us, commissioning both science and religion to look for deeper understanding. Of course, the impetus to trust can at times be diverted so as to lead to perversions not only in religion but also in the realm of science. But only a primordial trust can lead human minds to undertake the adventure of exploring the universe—as well as infinite mystery—in the first place.

I am emphasizing our ineradicable inclination to trust for two reasons. First, it shows clearly that the new atheistic attempts to cleanse human consciousness of faith are absurd and doomed to failure. Harris, for example, proposes that the removal of all faith is essential if reason is to reign supreme. But he cannot eliminate all traces of faith even from his own mind. As he undertakes his passionate quest to divest the world of faith, he first has to *believe* that the real world is rational, that truth is something to be valued and respected, and that his own mind is of such integrity that it can grasp meaning and make valid claims to truth. This trusting component is usually tacit and seldom explicit, but it is a powerful presence nonetheless. Our expert atheists have obviously failed to notice it even as it drives their own cognitional activity.

Second, by identifying the radical trust that underlies the cognitional life of every seeker and knower, we can locate the appropriate place of theology in its relation to science. Theology is not the answer to scientific questions, as the new atheists would like it to be—since this would make their job of destroying theology an easy one. Rather, theology responds to the question of whether the spontaneous trust that underlies every journey of inquiry, including science, is justifiable. Science cannot provide that justification since it already assumes that seeking understanding and truth is worthwhile. Nor can the new atheists provide the needed justification of their trust since they too simply take for granted that reality is intelligible and that truth is worth seeking.

So the really important question goes unanswered by science and the new atheists. Harris places enormous trust in his own power of reason, as the citation at the outset of this chapter reveals. He makes a tacit act of faith in his own critical intelligence. But he never provides us with a good reason as to why he should trust his mind to lead him and us to truth. In other words, he never justifies his enormous cognitional swagger. He simply believes blindly in the superior capacity of his own mind to find truth with a facility and certainty that people misguided by religious faith do not possess. In order to be a reliable guide for the rest of us, he has to trust that his mind can put us in touch with the real world. But why should he trust his mind at all, especially given the view of the natural world out of which his mind and ours is said to have evolved?

The new atheists' own belief system, scientific naturalism, logically undermines cognitional confidence, even if it does not necessarily do so psychologically. Since our minds are said to have evolved gradually from a mindless state of nature, why should we trust these same minds to put us in touch with reality? Where and how did they acquire such an exquisite competence, especially given the lowliness of their origins in nature? True, evolutionary science has a plausible explanation for why our minds are adaptive, but that is not enough to justify the spontaneous trust we have in our minds to put us in touch with reality or truth. In fact, we should instead distrust our cognitional activity if evolution is the ultimate causal factor involved in the making of minds. Since evolution is itself understood to be a mindless process, why does the scientific naturalist trust it to be good at anything but adapting?

In order to justify our cognitional confidence, something in addition to evolution must be going on during the gradual emergence of mind in natural history. For if our minds are nothing but the accidental outcome of a mindless evolutionary process, why should we trust them at all? A Darwinian account of the mind's critical capacities—factual though such a narrative might be—is not enough to ground the confidence we place in our cognitional powers. Darwin himself would agree. Writing to one of his friends, he agonized over whether the theory of natural selection, if we take it seriously and consistently, might not undermine the actual trust we have in our mind's capacity to understand and know reality. "With me the horrid doubt always arises," he admits, "whether the convictions of man's mind, which has been developed from the mind of the lower animals, are of any value or at all trustworthy. Would any one trust in the convictions of a monkey's mind, if there are any convictions in such a mind?"[8]

So evolutionary biology, the scientific naturalist's final court of appeal, is not enough. Mind has to be more than an adaptive mechanism in order to merit our trust. Biology, after all, has demonstrated that many adaptations in life are pure deceptions. Or, as another kind of evolutionary speculation would claim, the emergence of the human mind in evolution is the outcome of a series of accidents. That account is not enough to inspire confidence either. Moreover, social science has shown that the shifting winds of culture and society are not enough, at least by themselves, to validate the confidence we have in our minds to understand and know what is true and what is not. Under any purely naturalistic interpretation there is insufficient reason for trusting our minds. I have every reason to believe that our minds evolved too, and I fully embrace evolutionary biology. But I also trust my mind, and evolutionary science alone cannot justify that trust.[9]

## THEOLOGY AND THE QUEST FOR TRUTH

Theology can provide a very good answer to why we can trust our minds. We can trust them because, prior to any process of reasoning or empirical inquiry, each of us, simply by virtue of being or existing, is already encompassed by infinite Being, Meaning, Truth, Goodness, and Beauty. We awaken only slowly and obscurely into this unfathomably deep and liberating environment and are bathed in it all our days. We cannot focus on it, and we may not even notice it at all since, like fish in a river, we are so deeply immersed in it. But we may trust our capacity to search for meaning, truth, goodness, and beauty because these have already beckoned and begun to carry us away. Faith, at bottom, is our gracious and enlivening assent to this momentous invitation.

How, then, can we justify our cognitional confidence? Not by looking back scientifically at what our minds evolved from, informative as that may be, but only by looking forward toward the infinite meaning and truth looming elusively on the horizon. Simply by reaching toward the fullness of being, truth, goodness, and beauty, we are already in its grasp. This is the true ground of our cognitional confidence, and faith and trust allow us to be drawn toward that horizon in the first place. As we entrust ourselves to the call of being and truth, our minds are already being ennobled by the excellence of the goal toward which they are moved. As our minds are being drawn toward truth, these minds already partake of that for which they hunger. This is what gives our minds the confidence they need to search for truth.

The undeniable trust that empowers our search for understanding and truth does not show up in the daylight arena of objects on which scientists can focus. This trust arises from the deepest and most hidden recesses of our consciousness, at a level of depth that we can never bring into clear focus since the very act of focusing cannot take place without it. But even if we cannot grasp meaning and truth in an absolute and final way, we can allow them to grasp us. In surrendering to meaning and truth we are performing an essentially religious act, one in which even the atheist is an unwitting participant.

Science is simply not wired to either detect or rule out the existence of God. God is not a hypothesis. Nevertheless, even though science itself cannot pick up any distinct traces of the divine, this does not mean that God is totally out of the mind's range. At a usually tacit level of awareness, both the atheist and the theist participate in a common faith. They both believe that reality is intelligible and that truth is worth seeking. What theology adds is that the existence of God—that is, of Infinite Being, Meaning, Truth, Goodness, and Beauty—provides an adequate justification of this belief, as well as an answer to the question of why the universe is intelligible at all. There is nothing unseemly about beginning intellectual inquiry by making this implicit profession of faith. What is unseemly, indeed irrational, is an attempt to cover up this faith and, at the same time, a refusal to look for an adequate justification of it.

Theology, therefore, does not compete with science by looking for evidence to support a paltry God hypothesis. On the contrary, theology—a term that I am using in the sense of a Barth or Tillich—rightly objects to the atheists' device of collapsing the mystery of God into a set of propositions that can compete with, and then lose out to, science. Theology simply does not have to play such a ridiculous game, nor does it have to stoop to the level of silliness implied in the atheists' caricatures. Dawkins and his associates declare that reference to God is unreasonable, but what is really unreasonable is their refusal to look for an ultimate explanation as to why the universe is intelligible, why truth is worth seeking, and why we can trust our minds as they reach toward deeper understanding and truth.

# 5
# *Why Do People Believe?*

Religion has run out of justifications. Thanks to the telescope and the microscope, it no longer offers an explanation of anything important.

—Christopher Hitchens (282)

If God does not exist, and theology is empty, there has to be a purely natural reason that a great majority of human beings are, and always have been, religious believers. And if faith is a purely natural phenomenon, then science has the job of providing its ultimate explanation. Not surprisingly, the new atheists have a vested interest in finding a scientific explanation of religious faith. If science can uncover a purely natural suite of reasons for why people believe, this discovery, at least as far as our critics are concerned, would spell the final defeat of theology. These days, therefore, they are understandably impressed by confident new proposals that the final explanation of faith, and indeed all religious behavior, will come not from theology but from evolutionary biology.

By faith, let us recall, the atheists mean "belief without evidence." "Faith is what credulity becomes," Sam Harris states, "when it finally achieves escape velocity from the constraints of terrestrial discourse—constraints like reasonableness, internal coherence, civility, and candor" (65). A theological explanation would claim that people have faith because at the core of their being, and not just in their minds, they have allowed themselves to be grasped by God. But Harris would find such an idea irrational. Richard Dawkins and Daniel Dennett agree with Harris, simply adding that Charles Darwin has given contemporary religious skeptics a powerful new tool—the idea of natural selection—to answer once and for all the question of why so many of us are willing to hand ourselves over to faith. Theological explanation is no longer needed.

Christopher Hitchens is happy to go along with the Darwinian account of faith, but his discussion of why most members of the human family are so weak as to believe in God or gods without evidence is neither evolutionist nor scientific. Hitchens is still so entranced by Freud and Marx that he settles for retreading the well-worn projection theory according to which religion is just wishful thinking and hence, as he puts it, "man-made." He fails to mention that as long ago as the sixth century BCE the poet Xenophanes surmised that we create the gods in our own image, and the claim has been made repeatedly, even by theologians. The Trappist mystic Thomas Merton, for example, noted that our images of God tell us more about ourselves than about God; the medieval monk Meister Eckhart prayed for God to deliver him from God. For Merton, Eckhart, and other religious thinkers, however, the fact that religion always requires human imagination is completely consistent with the possibility that faith is fundamentally, and simultaneously, a response to the reality of God. Sam Harris claims that the root cause of religion is simply our enigmatic and abysmal propensity for "faith." But as we have already seen, faith may also be understood as the state of allowing oneself to be drawn into the timeless and endless depth of being, meaning, goodness, truth, and beauty that theists call God.

Richard Dawkins and his philosophical shadow Daniel Dennett, however, profess to have delivered us once and for all from theological accounts of faith. In the absence of God, they insist, only a scientific account of faith and its many religious expressions is plausible (Dawkins 163–207).[1] But which of the many available sciences holds the key to what faith really is? Psychological and sociological theories of religion may have something to them, according to Dawkins, but these provide only proximate, not ultimate explanations. Likewise, Michael Shermer's speculation that the origin of religious faith can be found in the human need for pattern or meaning might be right, but it still fails to provide a fully naturalistic explanation of religion.[2] Finally the recent overblown attempts to explain the causes of religion in purely neuroscientific terms do not go deep enough to satisfy Dawkins either. Only evolutionary biology can provide an ultimate account of why people are religious, or as Robert Hinde has put it, why gods persist (Dawkins 166–72).[3]

Not long ago, most evolutionists were reluctant to study religion very closely, assuming that science was not wired to comprehend the mysterious worlds of which religious people speak. But evolutionary scientists have recently gained more confidence, and beginning some thirty to forty years ago several of them, most notably E. O. Wilson of Harvard, began to suppose that religion, along with all other manifestations of life, must be studied biologically. More recently Dawkins has theorized that evolutionary biology can provide a thoroughgoing explanation of religious thought and behavior (166–72). He and many other evolutionists propose to "naturalize" our understanding of religion in terms of Darwin's evolutionary theory. Applying Occam's razor, they wonder why anyone would ever resort to religious and theological accounts of faith if simpler, natural ones will do.[4]

In order to explain religious faith biologically, one must make two broad claims. First, human behavioral patterns and routine cognitional operations are inherited, in the same way that our basic anatomy is. Second, inheritance consists of populations of genes migrating from one generation to another. Genes, however, are spread out among related organisms, so that the idea of evolutionary fitness (which means the probability of reproducing) applies less to an individual organism than to the wider pool of genes shared among kin. This idea is known as "inclusive fitness," and it is fundamental to most evolutionary accounts of religion.[5]

The Darwinian psychologists and anthropologists whom Dawkins most admires claim that the human brain has aided the passing on of human genes only because it evolved to perform a variety of tasks essential to survival as far back as 2 million or more years ago. Human beings today have inherited a brain and pattern of responses that evolved long ago under circumstances markedly different from those people face today. But what is most puzzling and irritating to Dawkins is that our brains somewhere along the line developed a tendency to believe without evidence, and to create wild religious ideas, embellishing them with senseless rituals. To Dawkins religious faith is annoyingly antiquated and evil (308). But at the same time it is a stubbornly durable human tendency, and its curious persistence requires an explanation, especially at a time in human history when science should have cleansed culture of this huge embarrassment. Psychology and neuroscience are not enough to account for it, so we must dig deeper.

Since God does not exist and therefore cannot be the ultimate explanation of anything, how are we to make sense of faith and its persistence scientifically? We have no choice but to look for an evolutionary account. Religious habits are so deeply rooted in human mammals and are so prevalent that they need an explanation that goes deeper than culture. Perhaps, then, religion can best be explained in evolutionary terms as having promoted the survival and transmission of human genes during the course of our evolution. So gene survival, not God, is the ultimate explanation of religion. If our genes are to make it into future generations, they need to manufacture human organisms with just those traits that will reliably replicate them, and apparently one of these traits has been the attraction of our species to the God delusion and other fabrications of faith (Dawkins 164–65).

This evolutionary explanation of faith seems persuasive to many scientific naturalists today. However, as Dawkins correctly acknowledges, the exact way in which religion promotes survival is not quite so straightforward. Although religion may at times aid individual, group, and genetic survival directly, at other times it does not. Yet people remain religious anyway, even where faith fails to be adaptive. Some religious phenomena, such as celibacy and martyrdom, are not adaptive. In these cases, can the Darwinian view of life still be rescued by such evolutionary notions as kin selection? Perhaps the altruistic sacrifice of an individual organism's reproductive opportunities can have the effect of enhancing the survivability of a whole population of genes that the altruist shares with its relatives, group, or species.

This explanation is tempting, but Dawkins suspects that kin selection and other factors associated with gene-survival theory are also too simple to account for faith (172–79). They do not explain adequately the arbitrariness and utter insanity of so many religious fantasies that people believe in without any evidence. So how is the evolutionist going to account for the persistence of gods in an age of science? Doesn't the evolutionary explanation of religion break down completely at this point? Apparently realizing that it does, although without admitting it, Dawkins hands over the task of fully naturalizing religion to other experts, one of whom is the anthropologist Pascal Boyer.[6] The effect of passing the buck to Boyer is deeply ironic. After promising to provide a fully naturalistic account of religious faith, Dawkins ends up breaking almost completely away from Darwin. Together with Boyer he speculates that the brain does not have any specifically religious character after all. So, then, what is religious faith? It is an accidental by-product of cerebral systems that evolved for other purposes. Religious faith is "a misfiring of something useful," a Darwinian mistake! Here then we leave Darwin almost completely behind (188). The only important evolutionary thing left to be said, as Dawkins theorizes, is that religion is like a virus—parasitic on cognitive systems that had earlier been selected because of a survival value that had nothing to do with their capacity to be carriers of faith.

One such cognitive system was the ability of our remote biological ancestors to detect predators.[7] Organisms that lacked predator-detecting mechanisms could easily have been killed and eaten, so they had a low probability of surviving. On the other hand, those that were good at detecting predators were more likely to survive and pass on their genes to our more recent human ancestors. But what does this have to do with the question of why most of us are still so religious? Boyer's answer, endorsed by Dawkins, is that a brain endowed with modules or systems that allow it to detect unseen predators is a ready refuge for religious ideas. Brains designed by evolution to detect hidden predators already have the capacity to look around for hidden agencies of all kinds. We have inherited the kind of brains that can easily attract and cultivate ideas about those ridiculous hidden agents we call gods or God. Even though human persons today are not so preoccupied with detecting predators, we are still saddled with essentially the same brains as our hunter-gatherer forebears. Having an excitable agency detection system makes our brains congenial hosts to the parasitic illusions of religion, even in an age of science.[8]

Notice, then, that the connection of faith to evolution has now become so loose that the entire project of naturalizing religion is clearly at a point of crisis. By this point in his argument Dawkins is showing signs of realizing how inconsequential evolutionary biology is to the naturalist's project of exposing and throttling the nuisance of faith. Perhaps this is why he also attempts to refute, on logical rather than scientific grounds, the classical arguments for God's existence (77–109). That Dawkins even bothers to take this detour into philosophy supports my suspicion that, at some level of awareness, he realizes that Darwinian biology provides precious little support for his naturalistic account of faith. He realizes that his gene-survival theory is not enough to account for religion, so he looks also for non-scientific ways of refuting theistic belief.

However, as Dawkins takes one last look back at the failure of biology to say anything substantive about what religious faith really is, he notes that genes may still provide analogies for his novel and extremely controversial idea of "memes." Memes are abstract cultural units of information transmission to which Dawkins and Dennett, in runaway explanatory ebullience, now attribute the spreading of the religious "virus" from one brain to another. By the time Dawkins makes his scientifically curious switch to memetics, a move that Dennett surprisingly takes up as the foundation of his own understanding of religion, Darwin has been shoved out of the theory of faith's origin and persistence almost completely. By releasing religion from exhaustive Darwinian explanation, Dawkins is in effect expressing the difficulty the whole modern naturalistic project is having in completely debunking religious faith.[9]

Elsewhere I have provided much lengthier critiques of Dawkins's and Dennett's naturalistic accounts of faith.[10] But even the brief discussion here is enough to show that the blazing hatred Dawkins has for religion has, in the final analysis, very little to do with evolution. If Darwinian theory were exhaustively explanatory of religious faith, there would be little reason to complain about it. Religion in that case would be just one more instance of the clumsy creativity of nature, no more objectionable than vestigial organs. But for Dawkins religious faith is in every respect an ethically despicable development, so the blame must not fall on blind and morally innocent Darwinian mechanisms. For Dawkins, evolution itself is not evil but merely indifferent. The evil in religion must then be extraneous to the life process, and therefore outside the scope of biology to account for it.

The posture of outrage that Dawkins takes toward religion is indicative of how far the core of his critique is removed from the more relaxed assessment of religion by other evolutionary naturalists.[11] Most scholars of religion who have come under the spell of evolutionary explanations are not nearly as judgmental and embittered toward religious faith as Dawkins. In fact, most evolutionary debunkers of religion are rather indulgent, if somewhat condescending, toward their misguided fellow humans who happen to believe in God. Sometimes they even allow that, were it not for ancestral human brains given to manufacturing adaptive religious illusions, none of us would be here. So, three cheers for Darwin, and two for religion. Although in our devotion to God we are lying to ourselves, the lie is benign as long as it remains adaptive.[12] After all, were it not for the deceptive way in which religious belief made our human ancestors suckers for gene survival, even critics of faith would not exist. Maybe we should show much more respect for the noble lies of religious belief than Dawkins does.

## THEOLOGY AND THE ORIGIN OF FAITH

What response can the theologian make to these attempts to provide a Darwinian debunking of religious faith? I have no doubt that one way of understanding faith is to explore it through the tools of evolutionary science, and I am convinced that theology should encourage science to push evolutionary understanding as far as it can within the limits of scientific method. From a scientific point of view our capacity for religious faith has evolved like all other living phenomena, and biology can lend an interesting new light to religious studies. But, like almost everything else, religious phenomena also admit of a plurality of levels of explanation. The phony rivalry the new atheists posit between science and religion is the result of a myth, a myth that asserts—without any experimental evidence—that only a scientific frame of reference, or only what counts as "evidence" in scientific circles, can lead us reliably to truth.

Theology, unlike scientism, wagers that we can contact the deepest truths only by relaxing the will to control and allowing ourselves to be grasped by a deeper dimension of reality than ordinary experience or science can access by itself. The state of allowing ourselves to be grasped and carried away by this dimension of depth is at least part of what theology means by "faith." In spite of what their formal creed states, even scientific naturalists have had the experience of faith as understood in this fundamental sense.[13] To be more specific, they too have made a worshipful bow toward the unconditional value of truth. I have no doubt that Dawkins, Harris, and Hitchens feel empowered to issue their bold edicts only because they firmly *believe* they are serving the noble cause of truth seeking. They probably have not noticed that, in order to serve this cause, they have tacitly allowed themselves to be taken captive, as it were, by their love of truth, an undeniable value that functions for them as a timeless good that will outlast them and their own brief success. Should they express outrage at what I have just said, this passionate reaction likewise could be justified only by their appealing once again to the value of a deeper truth than they can find in my own reflections.

It is not too hard for any of us to notice that we are always being drawn toward deeper truth, even if we decide to run away from its attractive, but also disturbing, pull. If you find yourself questioning what I have just said, it is because you are allowing yourself to be drawn toward a yet deeper level of truth. So you prove my point. What I mean by faith, therefore, is precisely this dynamic state of allowing yourself to be carried along toward a deeper understanding and truth than you have mastered up to this point. People have faith, therefore, not only because faith is adaptive in an evolutionary sense, not only because faith serves the cause of gene survival, not only because of ultrasensitive predator detection cerebral systems inherited from our remote evolutionary ancestors, not only because they have a need for pattern and meaning, and not only because their parietal lobes are overly active. Without denying that any of these factors may be at work, one may justifiably add that people have faith also because they are being drawn toward a dimension of depth. In theological language they are being addressed by and responding to the infinite mystery of being, meaning, truth, goodness, and beauty that theistic faiths call God. Such a claim is in no way opposed to evolutionary accounts of religion. Contrary to Dawkins, religious faith no more conflicts with science than does his own surrender to the value of truth.

Generally speaking, faith is the state of being drawn toward or being grasped by something of utmost importance, by what Tillich calls "ultimate concern." Our ultimate concern can be identified by asking what it is that gives meaning, zest, and courage to our lives. What sustains us in moments of hardship, failure, guilt, and the realization of our perishability? What is it that might cause our lives to fall apart if it were suddenly missing? Is it another person? Our job or career? World peace? The advancing of justice? God? Or is it perhaps science or reason itself?[14]

Sam Harris appears to be the only one of the new atheists to have so much as cracked open a work by Tillich, and even after doing so he slams it shut immediately.[15] To take theology into account would not serve the purpose of Harris's protests, which are "aimed at the majority of the faithful, not at Tillich's blameless parish of one" (65). Instead of grappling with a challenging theological elucidation of faith, Harris thinks it would be better for the unenlightened masses not to hear what theology has to say on our topic at all. In his comments on Tillich he dumbs down the definition of faith to "belief without evidence," even though he knows that Tillich has rejected this definition as misleading and not worth defending.

I am not sure how most readers will react to this rhetorical strategy, but I think it deserves several comments. First, it logically undermines the intended universality of the new atheistic condemnation of faith. Even one white crow is enough to show that not all crows are black, so surely the existence of countless believers who reject the new atheists' simplistic definition of faith is enough to place in question the applicability of their critiques to a significant sector of the religious population. Second, the readership that does pay any attention to the new atheistic tracts will include very few of what Harris calls "the faithful." The terrorists and religious fanatics being targeted exist far out of the range of our three wrathful diagnosticians. Although the books under discussion have landed on bestseller lists, the number of readers who will have purchased and studied them is only a tiny segment of the world's population. Moreover, a sizable portion of their readers are people who already agree with them, or who have serious doubts about religious faith, while others are simply curious as to what the fuss is all about. Of course, Harris and the others can always respond that they are hunting down liberals and moderates for tolerating freedom of thought and faith. But it is hard to believe that, short of a new atheistic dictatorship, they seriously expect the world will ever be purged of freedom of faith.

If they are truly serious about ridding the world completely of faith, therefore, the new atheists should start by grappling with major theologians rather than trying to outflank them. To get rid of faith, the atheists—by their own admission—will sooner or later have to get rid of theology. Theology, they claim, by making room for any faith at all, makes possible the delusions that take over the minds of terrorists, yet the books I am treating here make not a single major assault on any prominent theologian. (Dawkins's pelting of Richard Swinburne is too weak to qualify.) Given all their bluster about the evils of theology, why do they wade only ankle deep in the shallows of religious illiteracy? A well-thought-out military strategy sooner or later has to confront the enemy at its strongest point, but each of our critics has avoided any such confrontation. Unlike the great leaders in war, these generals have decided to aim their assaults exclusively at the softest points in the wide world of faith.

Third, an encounter with a theologian like Tillich would help the atheists understand better the tacit dynamics of their own atheism. They would be able to see that their own criticism of faith arises not from a neutral objectivity that empties one's head of all a priori assumptions. The very passion of their protests erupts from the deep font of a native trust in reason, an "ultimate concern" that has grasped hold of them and to which they have surrendered in fiduciary reverence. In this sense they are as religious as anybody else, so they have not severed their ties with the rest of humanity after all.

Fourth, in their very worship of reason and science, the new atheists have succumbed to what Tillich understands as the main temptation of all faith, that of idolatry. Enthroning reason and science as our only access to truth is an almost perfect illustration of the absolutizing instinct that ultimately deadens the vital spirit of inquiry. Scientism and rationalism imprison human minds no less than the worship of idols keeps religious believers from developing a liberating relationship to the whole depth of being. Theologically speaking, reason, in order to avoid self-imprisonment, needs faith, not in Harris's but in Tillich's sense of the term, for faith is what keeps reason from absolutizing itself. By stirring us at every level of our existence, faith holds the frontiers of our consciousness open to the infinite. Faith reminds us of how limited science and reason are in their capacity to penetrate the richness, beauty, and depth of being. Deifying science and reason, as only a little understanding of history is able to show, is a sure way to wilt the world and shrivel our souls.[16]

# 6

# *Can We Be Good without God?*

Conduct is a by-product of religion—an inevitable by-product, but not the main point. Every great religious teacher has
revolted against the presentation of religion as a mere sanction
of rules of conduct. . . . The insistence upon rules of conduct
marks the ebb of religious fervor.
         —Alfred North Whitehead[1]

The opposite of sin is by no means virtue. . . . No, *the opposite
of sin is faith.*
         —Søren Kierkegaard[2]

People of faith have often insisted that in the absence of God
human morality would fall to pieces. If a good God exists, they
have reasoned, this gives our moral behavior a secure and eternal foundation. But if God does not exist, isn't everything permitted? Why would we want to behave ourselves, after all, if
there are no timeless standards of right and wrong? And isn't it
one of the essential functions of a deity to draw up, for all times
and places, a clear list of what is right and wrong, to issue rules
of conduct that we should obey unquestioningly, and then to
reward the good and punish the evil? And don't all religions
exist primarily to place moral constraints on humans, who
would otherwise act like animals? Moreover, if you accept
human evolution, hasn't it been religion, especially ethical
monotheism, that has lifted us out of the purely natural sphere
and allowed us to become a distinctively moral species?

Although many believers in God would answer these questions affirmatively, theologically speaking things have never
been quite so clear. In fact, understanding the relationship of
morality to religious belief has always been one of the more
challenging tasks of theology. However, as we have already

observed many times, the new atheists are not interested in theology, preferring instead to set it aside as though it does not
exist. As far as this chapter's topic is concerned, they are content to make two theologically unadorned declarations and
leave it at that: First, morality does not require belief in God.
Second, humans would behave much better without faith in
God, since, in Christopher Hitchens's words, "religion poisons
everything." Let us now look more closely at each of these two
claims and then, in a third section, ask why religions that claim
to be so good can often be so bad.


## DOES MORALITY REQUIRE BELIEF IN GOD?

There is a strategic reason why Richard Dawkins and the other
new atheists want readers to think that faith in God functions for
believers as a necessary sanction for rules of conduct. If one
begins with this broad premise, then an easy way to invalidate
theism is to show that morality has a purely natural explanation.
If we can be good without God, then a major stone in the pillar
of faith is removed, and complete collapse follows. In two of the
more revealing chapters (6 and 7) of *The God Delusion*, Dawkins
tries as hard as he can to convince readers that the main point of
the Bible should be, to use A. N. Whitehead's words, the "insistence upon rules of conduct." Apparently Dawkins thinks that
this is fundamentally what the Good Book is for, and he assumes
the rest of us should too. The Bible, Dawkins must have decided
long ago, is intended to be essentially a compendium of "rules
for living," either by direct instruction, as in the Ten Commandments, or by providing "role models" for our own behavior
(237–627). It has failed on both accounts, he argues. Hitchens
agrees with Dawkins and has nothing else to add, so my focus
here is primarily on the Oxford evolutionist.

As regards direct instructions for conduct, Dawkins himself,
with the help of several of his favorite Web sites, can come up
with a better set of commandments than Yahweh gave us,
including: "Enjoy your own sex life (so long as it damages

nobody else) and leave others to enjoy theirs in private whatever their inclinations, which are none of your business" (263–64). As for ethical role models, the Bible has no good ones to offer either, starting with God. God comes off as "arguably the most unpleasant character in all fiction: jealous and proud of it; a petty, unjust, unforgiving control-freak; a vindictive, blood-thirsty ethnic cleanser; a misogynistic, homophobic, racist, infanticidal, genocidal, filicidal, pestilential, megalomaniacal, sadomasochistic, capriciously malevolent bully" (31). No wonder Abraham, Noah, and Moses are such shady characters also. Just consider their role model.

Jesus is a "huge improvement," but his ethnocentrism is still a scandal, and his critical posture toward his own mother and siblings is not one to promote family values (250). Furthermore, the entire Christian drama of redemption is morally perverse: "If God wanted to forgive our sins, why not just forgive them, without having himself tortured and executed in payment—thereby, incidentally, condemning remote future generations of Jews to pogroms and persecution as 'Christ-killers': did that hereditary sin pass down in the semen too?" (253). Why, then, would anyone call the Bible a *good* book?

So, having first tried to convince us that the main point of biblical religion is to provide moral edification, and, second, having demonstrated that it has failed miserably in doing so, Dawkins's third and main task is to point out that in fact most of us do not stoop so low as to make the Bible the source and inspiration of our moral lives anyway. In this way he intends to emancipate morality completely from religion. In fact, however, Dawkins strays off course on all three counts, starting with his opening premise. Even though many theists may agree with Dawkins that morality is the main point of biblical religion, it is not. The main point is to have faith, trust, and hope in God. Morality is secondary, and the principle underlying biblical ethics is that our conduct should be shaped with respect to others by the trust that God's promise of ultimate liberation will eventually come to pass. When we fail to trust in a compelling and noble vision of human and cosmic destiny, we then make conduct the main point of religion. The result is hypocrisy, self-salvation, perfectionism, and the crushing of life out of people. These attitudes and actions come under severe criticism by the prophets, Jesus, Paul, and most Christian theologians.

Because he is wrong on the first claim in his argument, Dawkins cannot defend his second and third points either. Having acquired his most striking theological comments from the likes of comedian George Carlin, humorist writer Douglas Adams, and *The Skeptic Magazine,* Dawkins's discussion of morality and the Bible is a remarkable display of ignorance and foolish sarcasm. I do not enjoy speaking in such a blunt manner about any writer, but not to do so here would be evasive. What is most lamentable about Dawkins's discussion is that it completely misses the moral core of Judaism and Christianity, the emphasis on justice and what has come to be known as God's preferential option for the poor and disadvantaged. To maintain that we can understand modern and contemporary social justice, civil rights, and liberation movements without any reference to Amos, Hosea, Isaiah, Micah, Jesus, and other biblical prophets makes Dawkins's treatment of morality and faith almost unworthy of comment.

What does deserve comment, however, is Dawkins's attempt to explain morality as a purely natural phenomenon. If morality does not depend on religious faith, then how is one to explain it? Why are we moral beings at all? Although there are older psychological and sociological theories available, today the figure of Charles Darwin stands ready once again to provide the needed explanation. Dawkins seems quite certain that the modern biological synthesis of Darwin's notion of selection with the more recent field of genetics can demonstrate that human morality, no less than the behavior of other animals, is the product of impersonal evolutionary invention rather than a free human response to an eternal goodness. Briefly, his argument is that we humans are moral beings at this time in natural history not because of any direct or indirect revelation by God of moral absolutes, but because our genes long ago fashioned human organisms whose virtuous behavior increased the probability that their genes would survive into future generations. In this way Darwinian biology provides the ultimate explanation of morality.

As we saw in the previous chapter, Dawkins and many other evolutionists have concluded that natural selection applies more precisely to the population of genes shared by members of a species than to individual organisms.[3] Biology indicates that we are moral because being good has contributed to human gene survival. Thus, no need for theological accounts exists.[4] According to the major religious traditions, altruism is the high point of moral existence, and selfless love especially convinces believers of the divine origin of human ethics. But evolutionists today think they can trace the origin of such precious virtues to unintended, accidental genetic occurrences that programmed some of our ancestors to be more cooperative and altruistic than others. Ancestral populations in which plenty of genes for cooperative and generous behavior were spread around had a better chance of surviving and reproducing than those not so enriched. Gene survival, not God, is the ultimate source of our moral instincts.

Altruism emerged at least faintly much earlier in evolution than humans did, and something like morality is already present in the mutual "cooperation" observable, for example, in ant colonies. Technically "altruism" in evolutionary biology means putting one's own genetic future at risk for the sake of the survival of the larger population of genes one shares with one's kin. For example, in ant colonies the "workers" will not pass on their own genes since they are sterile, but their self-sacrifice contributes to the survival of the whole colony and thus to inclusive fitness. "A single ant or honey bee," Matt Ridley notes, "is as feeble and doomed as a severed finger. Attached to its colony, though, it is as useful as a thumb. It serves the greater good of its colony, sacrificing its reproduction and risking its life on behalf of the colony."[5]

Instances of this kind of altruism abound in the animal kingdom where it is a purely natural evolutionary development. So the fact that altruism and self-sacrifice occur also in the human species does not require a theological underpinning any more than does cooperation in the world of social insects. If ants don't need God to be dutiful, why should we? Morality is purely natural, so even our highest moral ideals have not descended from on high. Religious believers are under the illusion that moral imperatives have their origin in the mind of a divine lawgiver, and this gives our precepts a fictitious aura of authority, but from a Darwinian point of view human morality is a purely natural outcome of our genes' need for immortality. It may *seem* that when we are virtuous we are motivated by eternal values, but Dawkins knows better. It is not God, but genes that are orchestrating the entire drama of ethical existence.

Dawkins realizes, of course, that moral life is much more complicated than animal behavior and that cultural factors are also important in shaping ethical life. Still, he remains adamant that morality is ultimately natural rather than divine in origin. At this point, however, his argument suddenly falls apart. As in his evolutionary "explanation" of religion, Dawkins begins by promising a fully naturalistic theory, but then he proceeds to modulate his promise of Darwinian elucidation to a point where in the end biology has very little to do with human virtue either. Dawkins eventually admits—in a colossal understatement—that evolutionists should not "mis-state the reach of natural selection" (220). All of a sudden he confesses that human characteristics that at one time served the cause of gene survival "sometimes misfire," in which case they may no longer promote gene survival (220). For example, an intelligent couple may engage in sexual activity even though they realize that, if the woman is taking the birth control pill, it will not lead to procreation. Their exercise of sexual instinct is an evolutionary "misfiring," a "by-product," a "mistake." For Dawkins, these terms have no pejorative connotations for there are a host of "blessed" Darwinian misfirings or mistakes in human behavior. Indeed, one of these is "the urge to kindness—to altruism, to generosity, to empathy, to pity" (221). In other words, natural selection at this juncture in Dawkins's exposition turns out to have little or nothing to do with virtue except to have guaranteed the survival of organic features that can misfire in the direction of ethical or, for that matter, unethical behavior.

By this point in Dawkins's argument, natural selection has become about as explanatory of human virtue as the chemical laws that bond ink to paper explain what I am writing on this page. In order for you to read this page the chemical "laws" relating to ink's bonding with paper have to keep on working reliably and predictably. But the actual content of what I am writing is not determined or explained by the science of chemistry. Likewise, in the transmission of moral values from one generation to another, the biological "laws" of genetic inheritance are at work shaping organisms capable of moral behavior. But if Dawkins is right about Darwinian misfiring, then the actual content of our moral reflection and decision lies completely outside the scope of Darwinian explication after all. In the light of such a huge reservation it is hard to believe that Dawkins still wants readers to agree that he has provided anything approximating a fully evolutionary explanation of morality.

Not only does Dawkins leave us still looking for the evolutionary account of morality he had promised, but he also illustrates the logical self-contradiction into which any attempt to give a purely scientific justification of morality eventually leads. Evolutionary insights into the story of how morality emerged in natural history may not be wrong as far as they go, but they do not work well if taken as adequate or final explanation. As one who professes to be guided by lofty moral ideals, loftier even than any he can find in religion, Dawkins finds himself in a situation where his own moral indictment of religious faith has no firm justification if the values or standards by which he renders his judgments can themselves be fully explained in evolutionary terms. After all, a blind, indifferent, and amoral natural process, which is how Dawkins has always characterized evolution, can hardly explain why justice, love, and the pursuit of truth are now unconditionally binding virtues.

Perhaps, though, Dawkins implicitly acknowledges the problem here and wants to account for his own valuations in terms of what he calls Darwinian mistakes, misfirings, or by-products. If so, as noted above, he has thereby in effect abandoned the project of naturalistic justification of morality and is faced with the even more daunting task of showing how one kind of misfiring is better than another. For at the stage of misfiring, Dawkins watches the rockets of morality and religion suddenly jettison their evolutionary booster and separate themselves cleanly from natural history. Here in effect Dawkins unconsciously falls back into the very dualism of nature and human existence that naturalism deliberately tries to disown. As long as he formally insists that all virtue can be accounted for ultimately in a purely natural and specifically Darwinian manner, the question remains as to where along the way the values he appeals to in his attack on religion acquired their authority. It does not help matters to claim subsequently that purely human creativity determines our moral values, since their cultural relativity still raises questions about how these values can avoid the aura of arbitrariness.

## DOES RELIGION POISON EVERYTHING?

"How Religion Poisons Everything" is the subtitle of Christopher Hitchens's new book *God Is Not Great*. The religion of which that author and the other new atheists speak is mostly monotheism, the strict belief by Judaism, Islam, and Christianity in one God. Other faiths are mentioned occasionally, but it is especially the toxicity of the God religions that the new atheists are attacking. The catalog of evils committed under the umbrella of theistic faiths is a long one, and the writings of Hitchens, Dawkins, and Harris could well serve as an examination of conscience by those of us who think of God as infinite goodness, self-giving love, the ground of our freedom, the author of life, and our ultimate destiny. Not everybody thinks of God in such terms, and it could be enlightening to find out why.

For now I would just say that there is no point in denying that people can be very moral without believing in God. Nor is there any point in denying that religions have been invoked in support of some of the most abysmal kinds of immorality. Still the real issue, raised but not answered by Dawkins, is how to justify our moral precepts so that we are bound by them unconditionally. The rhetorical impact that Hitchens's popular book has made is due mainly to its appeal to the reader's own sense of moral outrage. But in stating that religion poisons everything, that biblical monotheism is the cause of untold evils, and that God is not great, Hitchens thinks of himself as standing on a mountain higher than Sinai. Careful readers want to know how he came to occupy these heights and where the rest of us can gain the stamina to climb up there with him.

The books that have captured our attention here fairly shriek with passionate protest against the evils wrought in the name of monotheism. But the vehemence of such strong condemnation of wrongness can arise only from a secure sense of rightness. So what is the ground and source of the new atheists' sense of rightness? Is it simply a social, cultural, and historical consensus? If so, how do we know that this consensus is justifiable? After all, Nazism and anti-Semitism draw their authority also from a social consensus.

Or is Darwinian natural selection sufficient justification for the moral absolutes that ground the atheists' sense of outrage against the evils of faith? If so, how can the amoral process of natural selection become the ultimate court of appeal for what is moral? Even if our ethical instincts evolved by natural selection, we still have to explain why we are obliged to obey them here and now, especially since they may be evolutionary "misfirings." Moreover, our immoral instincts, such as cheating, lying, and even killing, may also be said to have been adaptive evolutionary traits. Unfortunately, experiments in social Darwinism have tried to make survival of the fittest the criterion of what is morally right, an approach that has been soundly rejected by every respected ethicist today. Our new atheists will not want to go down this road either.

So how can the atheist find a solid justification of ethical values? In the absence of God, as Harris conjectures, we can fall back on reason alone to explain what our obligations are and why we should heed them. Yet, even apart from the historical naiveté of such a proposal, this rationale simply leads us back to a more fundamental question: why should we trust our reasoning abilities either? If the human mind evolved by Darwinian selection in the same way as every other trait we possess, we still have to be able to justify our trust in its cognitional capacity—its ability to put us in touch with truth—in some other way than through biology alone. Evolution may account for why our minds are adaptive, but not necessarily for why they are reasonable. Harris undoubtedly places enormous confidence in his own cognitional abilities, but a naturalistic worldview by itself cannot justify that presumption. Harris, like Dawkins, fails to explain why he can trust his own mind if its ultimate explanation is the mindless, irrational process of natural selection. If our intelligence can be ultimately understood in evolutionary terms, where and how did it acquire the assurance that leads us to trust it spontaneously?

Completely oblivious to this question, Harris still insists that the sense of rightness that backs up his moral animus against faith can be justified only by reason, not by any content originating in a faith tradition. Reason alone is the ultimate source, foundation, and justification of ethics. But his own reasoning faculties should at least have made him realize that it is a leap of faith that has led him to trust in reason—a trust that not everybody shares to the same extent that he does. He has yet to tell us what is so special about his or anybody else's mind that we should simply entrust ourselves to it.

If there is any truth to a theological understanding of reality, on the other hand, it can elegantly justify both the trust we have in our minds and the sense of rightness that stands behind our moral protest. We may trust our longing for understanding since even to ask a proper question our minds already have to be immersed in reality's inherent intelligibility. In a silent way, the intelligibility that gives coherence to nature invites our inquiry and opens up our minds to do science and undertake other forms of inquiry. And we can trust our search for right understanding ultimately because our minds have already been taken captive by a truthfulness that inheres in things, a truthfulness that we cannot possess but which possesses us. Likewise, we can trust our sense of outrage at evil ultimately because we are already grasped by a goodness that is not made by ourselves, or by our genes, but which is the silent and unobtrusive goal of all our moral striving. Meaning, Truth, and Goodness are all names for the ultimate and endless horizon of Being in which our minds first awaken and our longing for rightness blossoms into virtue. The name theology gives to this ever-present context of all existence, thought, and action is "God." And the name for our trustful surrender to this mystery is known as "faith."

Faith, as theology uses the term, is neither an irrational leap nor "belief without evidence." It is an adventurous movement of trust that opens reason up to its appropriate living space, namely, the inexhaustibly deep dimension of Being, Meaning, Truth, and Goodness. Faith is not the enemy of reason but its cutting edge. Faith is what keeps reason from turning in on itself and suffocating in its own self-enclosure. Faith is what opens our minds to the infinite horizon in which alone reason can breathe freely and in which action can gain direction. Reason requires a world much larger than the one that mere rationalism or scientific naturalism is able to provide. Without the clearing made by faith, reason withers, and conduct has no calling. Faith is what gives reason a future, and morality a meaning.

## WHEN RELIGIONS GO BAD

The new atheist literature itself provides testimony to the common human expectation that faith in God is not supposed to go bad. There is no other way to interpret the shock, sense of scandal, and enraged accusation that the atheists pour forth toward faith in God. Unless they too expected theism to do a better job at making us a moral species, they would not be so upset. One of the standout features of the new atheism is its highly moralistic repudiation of the evil deeds, programs, and policies executed under the sponsorship of religion and its institutions. This criticism is also important for highlighting the hypocrisy that keeps people of faith from acknowledging the evils of their own religions. In spite of the new atheism's scholarly narrowness, its one-sidedness, and its many exaggerations, it is not altogether without truth and value. Its importance consists primarily in reminding readers of what happens when religions take themselves too seriously, enthroning themselves in the place of the infinite mystery into which they are supposed to initiate us. Religion and theology, of all human enterprises, are the most prone to self-absolutizing—in other words, to idolatry. As theologian Paul Tillich says, "[The] idea that the human mind is a perpetual manufacturer of idols is one of the deepest things which can be said about our thinking of God. Even orthodox theology very often is nothing other than idolatry."[6] Religions and theologies, therefore, are most compelling when they face up to, and express heartfelt contrition for, the damage their sins of self-absolutizing have wrought. Idolatry is what makes religions go bad.

The antidote to idolatry, however, is not atheism but faith. If the Absolute is disposed of officially, as the new atheists would prefer, the idol factory known as the human heart will not automatically shut down. Instead it will work overtime to fill the void with something more manageable, including science and reason. Science and reason are important ways to truth also, but they can at times be adored so devoutly that their bright lights blind us to deeper and darker regions of reality that can be reached only through nonscientific ways of knowing.[7] Faith, as Harris himself comes close to recognizing at times, does indeed arise from a never-satisfied craving, a craving to be filled with something proportionate to its passion for infinity. Harris is also right in noticing that this abyss at the core of our being can become clogged with almost any kind of content, including the most destructive religious fantasies or, in Dawkins's terms, God delusions. But what is most objectionable is not that there is no "evidence" for these fictions, as Harris complains. What is most objectionable—and even more deeply fictitious than Harris is aware—is our pretense that the content we stuff into the caverns of our hearts is always worthy of our worship. And on this point atheists no less than theists need to examine what has captured their trust and filled the hole in their hearts.

# 7

## Is God Personal?

The main source of the present-day conflicts between the spheres of religion and of science lies in [the] concept of a personal God.

—Albert Einstein[1]

One of the main obstacles to belief in God, at least for scientifically educated people today, is that God is usually thought of as personal. That God is personal is an essential teaching of Christianity, Judaism, and Islam. But not all traditional religions and belief systems have been comfortable clothing ultimate reality in the lowly apparel of feeling, care, responsiveness, love, anger, and so on. After Charles Darwin and Albert Einstein, the idea of a personal God may be harder than ever to swallow. For many evolutionists the ruthlessness implied in Darwin's notion of natural selection has apparently stripped the universe of any connection to a caring, providential God. And Einstein speaks for countless scientists and philosophers by insisting firmly that the lawfulness of nature is incompatible with trust in a personal, responsive deity. A God who can answer prayers might interrupt the closed, deterministic continuum of causes and effects that science requires in order to make right predictions. So if Darwin represents biology's demystification of life, Einstein represents the modern depersonalization of the universe by physics.

Physics provided the intellectual basis of scientific skepticism about God during much of the modern period, but today biology has taken its place. Evolution has become the scientific foundation of the new atheism as represented by Richard Dawkins and Daniel Dennett. Everything else that fuels their intellectual arguments against faith is secondary. Harris and Hitchens, for their part, simply take the Darwinian debunking of faith for granted without giving any evidence that they have thought much about it. But for Dawkins and Dennett, Darwinian science is as secure a support for atheism as one can find in intellectual history. In *The Blind Watchmaker* (1986) Dawkins wrote that, prior to Darwin's *Origin of Species,* one might have had an alibi for not being an atheist, but after Darwin no excuse remains. Darwin destroyed every reason people formerly had for belief in a Creator who designed and cares about life in the universe. *The God Delusion* assumes the same but adds that evolutionary biology is the ultimate explanation of religion and morality. Over a decade ago Dennett's book *Darwin's Dangerous Idea* argued that evolution's blind and impersonal way of creating life's diversity and complexity is irreconcilable with theistic faith. Now *Breaking the Spell* attempts to unfold in even more detail Dennett's belief that Darwinian biology holds the key to deep understanding of why humans are religious.

Dawkins, angrier than Dennett, adds that Darwinian biology exposes the idea of a personal God as not only intellectually but also morally offensive. Any creator who would be responsible for the suffering and struggle involved in the emergence of species hardly seems to be personally interested in the world. Darwin's own observations led him to doubt that the universe could have been created by a caring and responsive God. And, although Darwin himself was never an outright atheist, many evolutionists today agree with Dawkins and Dennett that it is impossible to reconcile belief in a personal God with the randomness, blind selection, struggle, waste, and lethargic unfolding of life on Earth during the last 4 billion years. Evolutionary biology provides all the proof they need that the universe lies beyond the pale of providence.

Meanwhile the idea of a responsive God has also been challenged for several centuries by influential philosophical interpretations of physics. Einstein's dismissal of a personal God is hardly unique since physics had long been able to dispense with that "hypothesis." Einstein talked a lot about God, and he even spoke of himself as a "religious" person. But he considered himself religious only to the extent that he had a strong sense of cosmic mystery and a passionate conviction that we need to commit ourselves to superpersonal values. He was convinced that a religious devotion to truth, for example, is essential to good science, which is what he meant when he said that science without religion is lame. But in no sense did he endorse theistic faith. His oft-quoted line, "God does not play at dice with the universe," has sometimes led to the mistaken supposition that Einstein was a theist of a sort, but by this unfortunate expression he was simply stating his firm belief that the universe is lawful and intelligible, not that it is in any sense grounded in a compassionate personal God. If physical laws are to be perfectly steady and free of caprice, then there can be no personal deity that can conceivably act or intervene in the natural world. This is why, for Einstein, the idea of a personal God is the main cause of conflicts between science and religion.[2] The new atheists eagerly second this sentiment.

Nevertheless, most human beings are religious in one way or another, and many atheists now agree that "spirituality" is healthy. Even Sam Harris, who wonders whether anybody has ever been as convinced an atheist as himself, thinks that a "spirituality" within the context of a purely naturalistic worldview is essential. Some scientific naturalists allow that the "mystery" of the universe laid open by science is inspiration enough to arouse a religious kind of devotion. In fact, Einstein thought of himself as a religious person partly because of his appreciation of the "mystery" that enshrouds the universe, especially the mystery of why the universe is intelligible at all. As long as the welcoming depths of mystery motivate the scientist to keep traveling along on the road of discovery, there can be no conflict of science with a purely "mystical" religion. Many other scientists today also think of themselves as religious in this nontheistic sense. The mysterious silence of the cosmos is enough to fill their hearts, and it has the added advantage of being easy to reconcile with the lawful, impersonal universe of physics.[3]

Einstein thought the universe, in order to be compatible with science, has to be impersonal—that is, impervious to any acts of intervention by a personal God. If the universe were open to unpredictable divine actions, miracles, or responses to our prayers, this would put limits on, and even undermine, the predictive power of science. Recently the renowned physicist Steven Weinberg, cited approvingly by Dawkins, has echoed Einstein's convictions about the impersonality of the cosmos. He surmises that physics may be on the brink of discovering a "final theory" that will lay open the "fundamental" dimensions of the cosmos. When physical science arrives at the basement of all being, little chance exists that any footprints of a divine Friend will be visible there.[4] However, Weinberg is disappointed that Einstein is willing to refer to himself as a religious man, and Dawkins is inclined to agree with Weinberg on this point. Since religion in Western culture usually entails belief in an *interested* God it could be misleading for an atheist to embrace terms such as "God" and "religion." Instead, the scientific atheist should accept the meaning that the term "religion" has for most people, in the West at least—namely, belief in a distinct, personal, transcendent, divine being, endowed with intelligence, will, feelings, intentions, and responsiveness. Atheists need to be completely candid so as not to make themselves seem less opposed to religion than they really are when they deny the existence of God.[5]

So, according to Weinberg, we should renounce theism not only for Darwinian reasons but also because physics is in the process of finishing up its modern project of desacralizing the natural world. Contrary to those who think contemporary physics is in the process of remystifying the world, Weinberg is adamant in claiming just the opposite. Still, he is not ashamed to admit that it would be comforting if an interested, personal God did exist. But in the absence of evidence, honesty requires that we resign ourselves—in the spirit of tragedy—to the impersonality of the cosmos. In his desire to draw out the real implications of a world shorn of God, Weinberg approaches what I earlier called hard-core atheism.[6]

## SCIENCE AND DIVINE PERSONALITY

In view of physical science's purging divine personality from the "fundamental" levels of cosmic reality, and considering biology's Darwinian expulsion of divine providence from the story of life, can the theological notion of a personal God still find an intellectually plausible place in contemporary educated discourse? I argue that it can, but only in conjunction with a critical discussion of scientific naturalism, the deeply self-contradictory worldview in which the new atheism is rooted.

First, contrary to Dawkins and Weinberg, it is not science that has dislodged the personality of God from nature. Rather, it is scientific naturalism that has done so. Scientific naturalists believe—since they cannot prove—that science is the privileged way to encounter the real world, that only scientifically available evidence counts, and that only scientific understanding and knowledge can be trusted. But since the only world that science is methodologically able to understand is an objective, impersonal set of quantifiable properties, this is the only world the strict scientific naturalist knows as well.

Scientific naturalism ignores the subjective side of nature, especially our own inner experience, as irrelevant to a fundamental understanding of the universe. Harris has several pages on the experience of subjectivity (207–14), but his discussion only solidifies his view of a world in which subjects have no real existence. Not only is subjectivity hiding from objective inquiry, "it actually disappears when looked for in a rigorous way" (214). Harris's fear and loathing of faith, of "belief without evidence," is consistent with scientific naturalism's tendency to exclude anything subjective, even one's own critical intelligence, from being an essential component of the real world. In Harris's scientistic belief system, faith can be ignored because it is firmly fastened to the subjective world that always hides from the glaring lights of science.

There is no problem, as I see it, with science's methodological device of focusing only on the objectifiable realm of being. Part of scientific method is to limit its vision and its claims to what is objectively "out there" for all to see. The problem is that the cognitive state of being transfixed by objects "out there" has become so much a part of modern intellectual sensibilities that the temptation arises to assume that there really is no "in here" at all. Or, if there is, it is a wispy lining on the underside of what is available only to objectivist scrutiny.

This methodological eclipsing of subjectivity and personality is proper to scientific understanding, but an exclusively objectivist method of knowing has negative ethical implications that the new atheists overlook when they blame religious faith for almost all of the world's ills. If everything real or worth talking about is an object accessible to scientific method, then the world of subjects and persons begins to slip out of sight and off the map of reality altogether. If a hammer is your only tool, then everything looks like a nail; if objectification is your only cognitional instrument, then everything looks like an object. The outcome is that the whole idea of "personality" becomes exiled from the realm of what scientific naturalists consider to be real. This banishment includes not only human persons, but also the subjectivity of other sentient beings, and if carried out consistently, the personality of God as well.

The depersonalizing of the universe by the postulate of objectivity—the claim that everything real belongs to the realm of objects—was virtually completed in the minds of "enlightened" thinkers long before Darwin and Einstein. The new atheism is only one of many dubious outcomes of this intellectual history. Once science left the laboratory and became a general habit of mind, the fact of personality gradually became lost to the consciousness of many "experts" altogether. Human organisms then came to seem like any other set of objects: as vulnerable to engineering, experimentation, and even elimination. The ethical implications are obvious. The new atheists all take great pains to convince readers that religion has been the cause of more evil, destruction, violence, and death than atheism has. I don't know quite how the two sides can be accurately compared, and considering the sorry records that both have chalked up, any measuring to see who comes out on top seems ludicrous. Nonetheless, it is not silly to ask about the implications various worldviews have in shaping the ethical sensibilities of people. Here I shall have to be content simply to ask readers to think carefully about the extent to which mass murders, pogroms, executions, wars, and exterminations, especially over the last century, have been facilitated by a worldview according to which not only the value but also the very reality of personality is up for question.

## THE MEANING OF EXPLANATION

My second critical observation is that the new atheists, following a tendency habitual to scientific naturalism, are confused about what it means to explain something. How this question relates to the idea of a personal God I discuss at the end of this chapter. For now I want to note that Dawkins and Dennett take it for granted that, if biology can explain morality and religion in natural terms, no room remains for theological explanation. In *Breaking the Spell* Dennett implies that if Darwinian biology can account for why people are religious, then theologians and those who believe in a personal God should give up their own attempts to do so. Almost everything the new atheists have written about the emptiness of theology is based on the gratuitous assumption that natural and theological accounts are deadly enemies.

This assumption overlooks the fact that multiple layers of understanding or explanation can exist. Almost everything in our experience, after all, admits of a plurality of levels of explanation in which the various accounts do not compete with one another. For example, one explanation of the page you are reading is that a printing press has stamped ink onto white paper.

Another is that the author intends to put certain ideas across. Still another explanation is that a publisher asked the author to write a critical response to the new atheism. Notice that these three layers all explain the page you are reading, but they are not competing with or contradicting one another. It makes no sense to argue, for example, that the page you are reading can be explained by the printing press rather than by the author's intention to write something. Nor does it make sense to say that this page exists because of the publisher's request rather than because the author wants to record some ideas. The distinct levels are noncompetitive and mutually compatible.

So also we do not have to agree with the new atheists that it is because of evolution, or any other natural explanation, rather than because of divine inspiration, that morality and religion exist. Just because religion and morality have a natural, neurological, psychological, or evolutionary explanation, it does not follow that a theological explanation is superfluous. Even if religion and morality have been adaptive—say, in the evolutionary sense of aiding the survival of human genes—theology is not necessarily wrong to claim at the same time that religion and morality exist because of a quiet divine invitation to each personal consciousness to reach beyond itself toward an infinite horizon of Meaning, Truth, Goodness, and Beauty. Such an explanation in no way competes with or rules out evolutionary and other scientific accounts of religion and morality. You do not have to choose between evolution and divine inspiration any more than you have to choose between the printing press and the author's intention when explaining the page you are reading.

Conversely, people of faith would be wrong to claim that religion and morality exist only because of divine persuasion rather than because of evolution. The page you are reading exists because of a printing press, because of the author's intention, and because of the publisher's request. In this explanatory hierarchy several levels coexist without mutual contradiction. Likewise one can logically maintain, all at the same time, that morality and religion exist because they have been biologically adaptive, because people are responding to a divine invitation, and because some human persons and communities experience a divine personal "Thou" addressing them from a dimension of depth to which science has no access.

Like other scientific naturalists, the new atheists suffer from a bad case of explanatory monism. That is, they assume that there is only one explanatory slot available, namely, the one shaped to look for physical causes, and this is enough. Scientism has shrunk their perspective to the point where it leaves only a narrow slit through which they view the complexity of the real world. The subjective, intentional, personal side of reality remains completely out of its sight. Consequently, when the new atheists examine phenomena as labyrinthine as religion and morality, they are fully satisfied if they can pare their explanation down to purely physical or biological terms. The outcome is about as illuminating as my telling you, the reader, that in order to understand this page it is enough to know that it came from a printing press. After all, doesn't Occam's razor specify that there is no point in looking for deeper explanations if simpler ones are available?

Occam's razor is one of Hitchens's favorite tools (68–71), but like other devices that he seems to have only recently discovered (such as the projection theory of religion), his use of it is unwieldy enough to be dangerous. I believe, then, that this is as good a place as any to comment on the way in which he and Dawkins use Occam's razor to slice the world down to manageable size. Occam's razor, named after William of Occam, a late medieval monk and philosopher, maintains that if there are multiple competing explanations available, we should choose the simplest one. Also known as the law of parsimony, the principle advises us that when we are trying to choose between competing hypotheses it is a good rule of thumb to take the one that makes the fewest assumptions, which seems like good advice. Why, then, Hitchens and Dawkins ask, should we look for a theological explanation if a natural (evolutionary) explanation of morality and religion is now available?

The new atheists all reason in this fashion. However, evolutionary and theological accounts lie on logically different levels, and hence they are noncompeting. So Occam's razor does not apply. If, like Dawkins and Hitchens, you prefer to approach all questions with an explanatory monism, then only a single causal slot is available, and in that case you have to decide between evolutionary science and theology. Accordingly, the new atheism advises you to take the natural explanation rather than the theological one if you want to understand morality and religion fully. But this would be as silly as being advised to choose the printing press rather than the author's intention or the publisher's request as the explanation of the page you are reading. Obviously in order to understand this page you have to assume that there are multiple levels of explanation available, but these levels complement rather than compete with one another. So it is with evolution and theology.[7]

Hitchens uses Occam's razor to choose between a theological explanation of religion and his not-so-original natural explanation that religion is "man-made." He simply assumes the presence of a forced option here. But the fact that biological and psychological factors are involved in the genesis of religion does not rule out the possibility that faith is awakened by the presence of God, a presence that scientific method is not interested in, but which may be experienced in other ways by those properly disposed. In faith's response to the loving presence and lure of God, the believer's brain chemistry, imagination, creativity, social belonging, past experience of parental figures and other persons, emotional life, need to be loved, and manifold other psychic factors are not pushed out of the way but instead are fully mobilized.

Theistic faith cannot make the idea of a personal God optional. Ultimate reality, the deepest dimension of being, cannot be less than personal if it is to command our reverence and worship. A necessary condition of our encounter with God is that we have already had the fully natural experience of interpersonal life. Experiencing ultimate reality only as an impersonal "It" rather than also as a personal "Thou" would leave the believer in God psychically, socially, and religiously unsatisfied. In one sense God is the ultimate in Being, Meaning, Goodness, and Beauty, but unless these impersonal absolutes are animated by the pulse of personality, they cannot attract personal beings at the deepest levels of our existence.

## DAWKINS AND EXPLANATION

Finally, this is also a good place to show how Dawkins's explanatory monism skews his response to the issue of God and design in nature. The big question for Dawkins is the same as the one that intelligent design (ID) theists are trying to answer: how to explain the incredible complexity and diversity in living organisms and cells. To the ID proponents, life's complexity is too elaborate to be attributed to natural causes alone. There must also be an "intelligent cause," a "master intelligence" that performs the miracle of bringing living complexity into existence out of physical and chemical simplicity.[8] So the question for both Dawkins and the ID proponents comes down to whether we should choose natural explanations of life's extraordinary complexity rather than theological explanations, or vice versa.

Dawkins, holding true to his flawed understanding of Occam's razor, finds the answer quite easy: choose the simpler hypothesis, the one that makes the fewest assumptions. That would be the naturalistic, Darwinian account, of course. All the scientist needs in order to explain life's complexity is the simple evolutionary recipe consisting of three ingredients: random variations or genetic mutations, blind natural selection of survivable variations, and an immense amount of time. The advantage of this purely natural recipe, and what gives it its appealing simplicity, is that it does not have to assume a preexisting personal intelligence to explain complexity. Chance plus blind selection plus deep time—this is all we need.

But let us invoke our analogy once again. For someone who does not know how to read, all that is needed to explain this page's existence is an awareness that a printing press caused it. Why complicate the simple elegance of that explanation by learning to read and then bringing in the fact that an author is trying to express a meaning on this page, and that the publisher has an even wider goal in mind? What Dawkins is in effect demanding is that his readers choose the printing-press explanation since it is simpler and more parsimonious than the author explanation (or the publisher explanation). But what Dawkins is overlooking is that these are not competing explanations and that Occam's razor applies only to competing accounts. Furthermore, William of Occam said that explanations should not be multiplied beyond necessity. Sometimes it is necessary to have a plurality of levels of explanation.

Dawkins's ideal of explanation begins with an unwarranted decree: There shall be no more than one explanatory slot![9] Then he tries to force the idea of God to play the role of a hypothesis just like those of science. That way he thinks he can compel theology to compete with and then be defeated by his "simpler" Darwinian explanation. Indeed this completely arbitrary decree of his—let us call it the postulate of explanatory monism—is the fundamental principle behind his uncompromising insistence that God is a hypothesis. It is the fundamental, but false, principle that underlies most of Dawkins's speculations about faith and God.

If you were illiterate and hence unable to read the meaning that can be expressed in print, it would be quite easy to convince you that the author's or publisher's intention is not a causal factor in the production of this page. As you examine how ink bonds with paper you would find at that level of analysis no physical evidence that there are more fundamental and more subtle levels of influence involved. Similarly, if someone is religiously or theologically unlettered, and has no capacity to look for deeper meanings in the natural world, it is easy to deny that life's complexity requires anything more than a Darwinian explanation.

Here again Dawkins seems to have learned the rules to his game from creationists and ID theists who also adopt the postulate of explanatory monism. They too are willing to think of God as a "hypothesis." It's just that for them the winner is God rather than Darwin. But the game's rules are the same as they are for

Dawkins: there shall be no more than one explanatory slot. Theology, however, does not have to play by these arbitrary rules, and fulminations such as *The God Delusion* are not going to persuade theologians to exchange richly textured understanding of the world for the shallowness of single-level explanation.

In keeping with his postulate of explanatory monism, Dawkins (147) also raises the pseudo-objection that if theologians are going to use God as an explanation of living complexity, then they have to take the next step and explain the existence and "complexity" of God (whatever "complexity" might mean as an attribute of God). The God hypothesis, Dawkins insists, makes too many initial assumptions, especially the assumption that there already exists an extremely complex intelligent, personal Designer named God who can then create immediately the complex design in cells and organisms. How then can theologians explain the existence of this God (147)?

I do not have the space here to unfold all the assumptions that must have gone into the begetting of this question. Let us just say that Dawkins seems willing to listen to theologians, provided we first agree with him that: (1) God, if God exists, is an instance of complex design; and (2) like any other instance of design the existence of God requires an explanation, such as the Darwinian one, in which complexity arises gradually out of physical simplicity by way of cumulative small changes over an immense period of time. For Dawkins this is the only way in which complex design could conceivably emerge.

Dawkins, of course, is free to define terms any way he wants, but theology does not have to accept his characterization of God. The God of theology is not an instance of complex design in Dawkins's sense of a composite put together over the course of time out of simpler components. Rather, God is the ultimate reason that there is the possibility of any complexity at all. For Dawkins the ultimate ground of complex design is *physical simplicity plus time plus gradual cumulative change*, and his quest for ultimate explanation comes to a dead end in this Darwinian formula. But theology has to probe deeper, seeking the ultimate explanation of the existence of a universe in which *physical simplicity plus time plus gradual cumulative change* can lead to complexity at all.

What Dawkins is demanding is that theology agree to drop its timeless understanding of God as the "ultimate ground of all being" and substitute for that understanding one in which God—if God exists—needs an explanation just like every other instance of complex design. That is, God would have to come into existence gradually out of a primordial simplicity. Here Dawkins is again assuming that there is a single explanatory slot available, the same slot that scientists fill with purely physical accounts of experimental outcomes. So God has to play by Dawkins's rules and become the outcome of a physical process that hypothetically preceded the existence of God. Needless to say, theology does not have to embrace the postulate of explanatory monism.

\* \* \*

Is this discussion relevant to the question of whether God is personal? Yes, because it shows that Einstein, when he forbade God to be personal, was making the same mistake Dawkins does about where to locate theological explanation in relation to science. Like most other scientific naturalists, Einstein was afraid that a responsive God can act in the world only by intruding into the natural continuum of causes and thus disturbing the lawfulness of physical reality. But God's personal wisdom, love, and responsiveness no more compete with physical causes than my publisher's request to write this book interferes with the chemical laws that bond ink to the paper on the page you are reading. The physical determinism, or lawfulness, of the lower levels in the hierarchy of explanations does not need to be suspended in order for the universe to be influenced by a personal God.

# 8

# Christian Theology
# and the New Atheism

The history of Christianity is principally a story of mankind's
misery and ignorance rather than of its requited love of God.
                                          —Sam Harris (106)

How extraordinarily stupid it is to defend Christianity. . . . To
defend something is always to discredit it.
                                          —Søren Kierkegaard[1]

The point of Christian theology, Pope John Paul II wrote in his
encyclical *Fides et Ratio,* is to explore the mystery of God's self-
emptying love. "The prime commitment of theology is the
understanding of God's *kenosis* [self-emptying], a grand and
mysterious truth for the human mind, which finds it incon-
ceivable that suffering and death can express a love which gives
itself and seeks nothing in return."[2] No theological radical
himself, John Paul expressed here what countless other Christian thinkers now agree is the radical message of Christian
faith. The God who for Christians became manifest in Jesus of
Nazareth is vulnerable, defenseless love, the same love that
Christians confess to be the ultimate environment, ground,
and destiny of all being.

Following the advice of Kierkegaard, however, in this final
chapter I do not try to defend this Christian understanding of
God against the assaults of the new atheists. It needs no defense
since it never comes up in their polemic. Moreover, the many
abuses committed in the name of the self-centered potentate—
Dawkins might say "monster"—that has often been substi-
tuted for Christianity's God do not deserve to be defended

92

anyway. As far as the existence of the self-giving love that Christians call God is concerned, nothing in the books by Dawkins, Harris, and Hitchens could be called a serious theological provocation. Sadly, the deepening of theology that has occurred in previous conversations between serious atheists and Christian thinkers has little chance of happening here. As examples of more fruitful conversations, I am thinking of how the theology of Paul Tillich was deepened by his encounter with the writings of Friedrich Nietzsche and atheistic existentialism; of Karl Barth with Ludwig Feuerbach; of Karl Rahner and Rudolf Bultmann with Martin Heidegger; of Jürgen Moltmann with Ernst Bloch; of Gustavo Gutiérrez with Karl Marx; and of many contemporary theologians with Jacques Derrida, Jacques Lacan, and Jürgen Habermas. At least the atheists on this list had enough understanding of theology to make conversation interesting and productive. In marked contrast, the level of theological discernment by the new atheists is too shallow and inaccurate even to begin such a conversation.

What might be worthy of theological attention, however, is the moral perfectionism that energizes the new atheism and makes it so appealing to some of its disciples. Sam Harris's heartfelt indignation against Christianity, as expressed in the citation above, is typical of the new atheists' arraignment of theistic faiths for their failure to actualize their own ethical ideals. It is certainly not hard for any impartial reader to agree that devotees of the theistic faiths have often failed miserably to practice what they preach. In the enormous sins of omission as well as commission by their members, the Abrahamic religions have undeniably deserved the justifiable wrath of the righteous. There is no lack of righteousness on the part of the trinity we have been listening to in the preceding chapters.

The scolding of religious abuse and mediocrity, however, was already a major motif in the prophetic voices that pestered the consciences of the citizens of ancient Israel and Judah. It would be hard to find in all the annals of atheism any more substantive denunciation of religious abuse than that memorialized in the words of Amos, Hosea, Isaiah, Jeremiah, Ezekiel,

Micah, and their ilk throughout the ages. With enormous force the prophets among us have repeatedly risen up in self-endangering revolt against the sanctimonious fat-cat religiosity of their own times. Without any attempt to prettify their outrage, they have roundly condemned their fellow believers, especially for failing to practice justice. In this prophetic tradition—of those who thirst after justice—Jesus of Nazareth was to discover his own identity and mission.

So it is curious that, unlike many serious atheists of the past, not one of the authors we have examined seems to be remotely aware of the biblical prophetic tradition, the moral core of Judaism and Christianity.[3] In contrast to much previous atheistic bashing of Christianity, the theme of social justice is hardly noticeable as an issue for Dawkins, Harris, and Hitchens. Dawkins does give an uneasy nod to one of the most prophetic figures of our time, Martin Luther King Jr. But he insists that King's message was "incidental" to his Christianity (271). Hitchens also feels obliged to mention King, but he claims that King's legacy "has very little to do with his professed theology" (180). Neither critic shows any sign of ever having read King's "Letter from Birmingham Jail." That landmark document in the civil rights movement clearly cites Jesus and the prophets as the most authoritative voices in support of what others had called the "extremism" of King's protests against the injustice of racism:

> Was not Jesus an extremist for love: "Love your enemies, bless them that curse you, do good to them that hate you, and pray for them which despitefully use you, and persecute you." Was not Amos an extremist for justice: "Let justice roll down like waters and righteousness like an ever-flowing stream." Was not Paul an extremist for the Christian gospel: "I bear in my body the marks of the Lord Jesus."[4]

This willful misunderstanding of King provides a prime example of the extent to which the new atheism will go to portray biblical faith as unambiguously evil. Were they to associate King with the prophetic tradition, it would credit the Bible with much more ethical goodness than they think it deserves. Incidentally, while Dawkins is taking pains to purify King from the contaminating influence of the Bible by linking him to Mohandas K. Gandhi—who, we are informed, was not a Christian (271)—Hitchens is busy discrediting Gandhi for connecting his message of liberation too closely to faith of any sort (184). Both authors contend that King would have been a more effective social liberator if he had never been exposed to Christianity and its Bible.

## PURITANISM

Concern with issues such as social justice and environmental responsibility are not important in the new atheists' critique of Christianity, as they have been for other atheists. Nevertheless, it is still in the name of morality that our three godless perfectionists send down their most energized bolts of lightning. In fact, from a Christian theological point of view, what stands out above everything else in the new atheism is its cognitional and ethical puritanism. Its proponents are so confident of having unimpeded access to truth and ethical rightness that they can now make a complete break from the intellectual and moral impurity of faith-crippled human beings up to this point. They claim in effect to have finally delivered our native rationality and capacity for moral discernment from centuries of thralldom to the ancient literature and Iron Age lunacy of Abrahamic religions. Intellectually, the new atheistic Puritanism takes the form of an uncompromising scientism that sanitizes our minds by scrubbing off all the griminess of faith. Ethically, the same puritanical obsession manifests itself in a promise to ground morality henceforth in a rationality cleansed by science of all ties to religiosity.

Ironically, the promoters of this neo-Puritanism seem to have no awareness that their own perfectionistic program has hardly purified itself of ancient dualistic mythic accretions that go back centuries before Christianity. The new atheists are not

the first cognoscenti to have promised salvation by pure knowledge, and the absence of any sense of paradox, irony, tolerance,
and ambiguity in their teachings is symptomatic of a persistent
human temptation to become obsessed with cognitional and
ethical purity at the expense of nuance and complexity.

This obsession itself stems from a sense of disembodiment
promulgated by the dualistic—some would say "Gnostic"—
mythology that has never been fully expurgated from Western
thought. I would suggest, therefore, that the cultural roots of the
new atheistic disgust with biblical faith lie not only in an uncrit-
ical academic strain of scientism but also in the same ancient
dualistic trends that still live on unconsciously in the puritanical
vision of reality.[5] As the great philosopher Paul Ricoeur has
shown, this puritanical vision goes back to ancient myths that
separated the soul (and later "mind") completely from matter
and bodiliness, a vision that Christianity has denounced from
the beginning, but so far obviously without complete success.[6]

The new atheistic puritanism is manifested most glaringly in
its moralistic indictment of the Scriptures sacred to Jews, Christians, and Muslims. These allegedly "holy" books, according to
our new perfectionists, are polluted in at least four ways: first, by
the simple fact of their antiquity; second, by their failure to provide true (that is, scientific) knowledge; third, by their tolerance
of rules of conduct and role models that fail to meet the new
atheists' standards of rightness; and, fourth, by their promotion
of faith.

Instead of distancing itself apologetically from this impeach-
ment, however, theology may reply that Christianity is guilty as
charged. All I would wish to add is that everywhere the new
atheists' ideal of purity causes them to see pollution, Christianity
sees embodiment. Christianity's vulnerable God is not detached
from the chaos of natural and historical processes. Its God is
unabashedly incarnate; fully enfleshed in the world; and inti-
mately related to its becoming, antiquity, creativity, pain, uncer-
tainty, mortality, weaknesses, and hopes.

Most scandalous to the puritanical mind-set of the new
atheistic exegetes is that the God of the Bible seems so erratic,

jealous, angry, violent, legalistic, and judgmental. (It goes unmentioned that in other moods Yahweh is slow to anger, lenient, loving, caring, and forgiving.) It is disgusting, especially to Dawkins and Hitchens, that biblical faith is so anthropomorphic. Measured by their puritanical standards, the Almighty should be above all such compromising associations with human characteristics. Moreover, if the Bible is supposed to be "written by God," as Harris puts it, why can't its Author come across as intellectually, scientifically, morally, and emotionally more respectable? Hitchens is so appalled that the Bible fails to live up to his perfectionistic portrait of the ideal divinity that he is forced to conclude that, alas, religion is something human beings "manufacture." The main reason for his writing *God Is Not Great* appears to be that of letting the rest of us in on his discovery.

## INCARNATION

In the previous chapter we saw that the very idea of a personal God as such, regardless of specific characteristics, is problematic to the new atheists, as it is to almost all scientific naturalists. However, it is hard to imagine how the reality of a divine mystery, if it exists at all, would capture the attention and allegiance of personal human beings if it presented itself as anything less than personal. Anthropomorphic imagery is offensive to a kind of Gnosticism that insists on the complete disassociation of faith from history, and of God from being involved in specific times, places, and events. But to an incarnational faith God is not detached from the world but instead absolutely related to it.[7] This relatedness cannot be brought home to religious persons by way of impersonal imagery.

If God is absolute self-giving love, as Christian faith proclaims, it would not be surprising that this love would humbly and hiddenly disclose itself to members of our species in the modest raiment of human personality. The Christian belief that God is fully present in Jesus the Christ means, at the very least, that God's perfection consists not of a self-purification from the ambiguity in nature's evolution or from the sinfulness in human history, but of an unequaled intimacy with the world in all of its struggles and iniquity. The goal of this intimacy is the lifting up or "divinization" of the world, but the point of departure for this adventure is a very unfinished and imperfect universe. Christian theology is not at all embarrassed that anthropomorphic imagery would be essential to the gradual self-revelation of God. To hold with Hitchens that religion is therefore "man-made" is only half the story. The other half is that it is God's intimacy with the world that evokes the "manufacture" by human persons of a truly revelatory personal imagery in the first place.

Theologically interpreted, not only biblical faith but also the long religious journey of our whole species is a series of responses to an invitation to intimacy by the inexhaustible mystery of God. But since no particular imagery can ever capture the fullness and depth of this elusive infinite mystery, humanity's religious search, including that of Christians, is never conclusive. Hence the many births and deaths of gods and goddesses throughout the ages is logically consistent with the quiet but constant presence and invitation of the Infinite. The divine invitation grasps us more than we grasp it, so we cannot subject it to our intellectual control. We can talk about it only in the imprecise yet luxuriant language of culturally conditioned symbols, analogies, and metaphors. But perhaps it is intellectual control that we want. If so, in our frustration that the divine mystery eludes scientific comprehension we are likely to interpret the unavailability of God as an infinite emptiness. The confusion of infinite fullness with endless emptiness is one of the essential marks of atheism.

However, the fact that religious icons come and go, or that early biblical symbolism of God is not to our tastes, is not enough to prove that the world's ultimate environment and final destiny is infinite nothingness. In fact, our perpetual religious discontent, and even our sincere frustration with religion as such, can occur only if our consciousness is already in the grasp of something more profound and far-reaching. If it were not, then there would be no basis for our iconoclastic protests. Sensitive souls in every period of religious history can grow weary of the unsatisfactory ways in which contemporary religions represent their ideal. Sometimes serious atheists might grow so weary of representations of the sacred that they denounce all religion as crude and vulgar. But even well-intentioned grievances against "God" or images of God can have no starch to them unless the complainants are already standing in deeper ground themselves. A good name for this deeper ground is God.

## THE TOLERANCE OF AMBIGUITY

In effect, therefore, the new atheists are demanding that religions either provide perfect representations of God (suitable to their tastes) or abandon images altogether, but Christianity tolerates ambiguity and imperfection in the Bible's struggle to imagine God. Why? Because the alternative is much worse, namely, an Absolute that remains eternally above the world's struggles in splendid isolation from the hopes, tragedies, sorrows, and struggles of weak human beings and the larger story of cosmic and biological evolution. Such a detached God would be an accurate reflection of the new atheists' moral ideal, but this would not be the God of Christian faith. In fact, from the point of view of the Bible's prophetic tradition, the puritanical God of splendid isolation would be the truly immoral "role model" for humans.

The new atheists' job description for the ideal deity calls for a Perfection purified not only of the vulgarity of tribal existence but also of contamination by human existence as such. The Christian God does not qualify. Christianity's intuition is that God is incarnate, that the Creator fully embraces the world in all of its imperfections, even to the point of becoming a child, eating with sinners, and experiencing death on a cross. Christian theology's advice to readers of those chapters in the Bible where God does not seem quite up to snuff morally is always to interpret everything in the Bible in light of its dominant themes of hope, liberation, incarnation, and God's self-emptying love. As soon as we let these main motifs out of sight we end up reading passages in literalist isolation, as Dawkins does when he comes up with his portrait of the monster God of the Old Testament. Reading certain passages in the Bible, including the Christian Scriptures, can be a dangerous and bewildering experience if one has not first gained some sense of the Bible's overarching themes. From a Christian theological point of view, perhaps the most important of these is that of freedom, which, along with the topic of God's promise and fidelity, binds most of the Bible's books into a coherence unnoticed by the new atheists. In their own deliverance from slavery and genocide the Hebrew people found the experiential basis of their symbolizing of God as Liberator, yet the close association of God with liberation, a defining feature of the Abrahamic traditions, is nowhere mentioned, let alone seriously discussed in the books we have been examining.[8]

One of the great benefits of taking a good college-level course in biblical literature, or of being part of a Bible study group informed by up-to-date scholarship, is that one can learn to read biblical texts in such a way that a major theme, say that of liberation, remains transparent in the background even while we are reading passages that may seem morally offensive when taken in isolation. For example, Hitchens cannot get over the story of God's command to Abraham to murder his son. "There is no softening the plain meaning of this frightful story," he moralizes (206). But it is Hitchens's plain reading of everything in the Bible that leads him and his fellow literalists to ignore the leitmotif of unconditional faith in a liberating God that underlies the story of Abraham and Isaac, as well as many other biblical narratives. Since Hitchens has already repudiated faith of any sort, the only value the Bible could possibly have for him is that of moral instruction. Once the florid motifs of promise, fidelity, and liberation are blanched from the pages of Scripture, as they are in Hitchens's avowedly "plain" reading of isolated texts, then the story of Abraham and Isaac becomes nothing more than a case study in bad behavior.

Similarly, Dawkins takes moral offense even at the Ten Commandments and the biblical proscription of graven images (237–48). Insisting that "the Bible is not the sort of book you should give your children to form their morals" (247), he fails to realize that the prohibition of idolatry in the Decalogue and the Prophets can be read as an expression of the Bible's fundamental theme of liberation—that we need not tie our lives to things that are too small for us. His derision of the Ten Commandments completely misses their covenantal and liberation-oriented context. Once these themes are washed out of his exegesis, nothing remains but arbitrary thou shalts and shalt nots. But this is fine with Dawkins since he wants his readers to join him in reducing the Bible to moral education. His hope is that, once readers get distracted into making that same assumption, they will agree with him that the Bible is such a failure at accomplishing what he thinks is its primary purpose that it is best for all of the rest of us to ignore it altogether.

From a Christian theological point of view, however, the main point of the Bible is not morality anyway, but that we should never lose trust that our lives, human history, and the universe itself are part of a momentously meaningful drama of liberation and the promise of ultimate fulfillment. Furthermore, the sense that our lives have a meaning, and that life is worth living in a spirit of trust, provides an energy and direction to moral aspiration that it would otherwise lack. According to the cumulative religious wisdom of our species, without a basic trust that the whole of being, including the universe itself, has a meaning, our ethical juices will eventually dry up for lack of nourishment. Yet the new atheism is doing everything it can to convince us that the universe is pointless and that in the end our lives are destined for nothingness as well—not the most favorable setting for the flourishing of our capacity for goodness.

The new atheists, one can be sure, will keep insisting that the Bible is not about meaning but about morality, as though the two were separable. But because Christian theology looks for meaning before it shapes its morality, it does not claim that everything in the Bible is of equal worth, morally speaking, anyway. In practice most Christian proclamation has allowed for a selective reading. The Bible includes frankly barbaric texts that nobody finds edifying. In fact, the liturgical life of the churches has routinely left out verses of Psalms and other writings that ask God to crush our enemies, for example.

Nevertheless, even the fact that certain texts over the course of time become irrelevant or offensive to our contemporary ethical tastes is completely consistent with the incarnational character of biblical faith. Rather than dwelling in a Platonic sanctuary above the terrors of history, the God of Christianity becomes embodied in events that are historically and culturally contingent. No doubt, a God whose identity gets so intertwined with specific times and places, as well as with suffering and death, has always been hard to swallow, even for many Christians. Many of Jesus' contemporaries were shocked that he mixed easily with people of ill repute, and so they questioned how he could be of God. Yet, in the spirit of a God who embraces ambiguity, Christianity decided fairly early in its history, though not without opposition, to include in the biblical canon those texts that Dawkins and Hitchens find contemptible. Both of these moralists may have enjoyed the company of Marcion, a heretic denounced by the early Christian church for teaching that the God of the Hebrew Scriptures could not possibly be the God of Jesus Christ.

The unspoken premise behind Hitchens's and Dawkins's disdain for the biblical way of imaging God is that it violates their implicit standards of moral and religious purity. But this idealism raises the question of how the new atheists themselves arrived at their own refined sense of good and evil. Harris tries to come to their rescue. He claims that our sense of right and wrong comes by way of a direct "intuition" untouched by time and historical existence. "The fact that we must rely on certain intuitions to answer ethical questions," he writes, "does not in the least suggest that there is anything insubstantial, ambiguous, or culturally contingent about ethical truth" (184). Just as he can arrive at true knowledge by way of science sterilized of faith, this new atheist can be transported into the realm of pure goodness by a faculty of intuition scoured clean of history and even bodiliness. How, then, can Christianity, with its sorry role model of a God in love with matter, time, history, bodiliness, and sinners, ever hope to measure up to such a standard of purity?

I should note that Christian theology throughout the centuries shares much of the blame for the fact that the new atheists' puritanical ideals became embedded in the mythic substructure of Western intellectual and popular culture. In fact, many dualists still reside among the ranks of Christian believers as well as those of the atheists, but this dualistic ideal has always existed in tension with the biblical foundations of Christianity. In the last several hundred years Christian theology has been gradually retrieving, though not without setbacks, its original and more adventurous belief that God is not to be sought apart from the material world, human embodiedness, and the ambiguities of historical existence. Thus, it is all the more fascinating that the new atheists are now taking Christianity to task by looking for support to the same conservative, puritanical, dualistic themes from which Christianity has been struggling to detach itself for centuries. Their combat with Christianity today is the latest chapter in an almost perennial struggle between two ancient religious ideals: the puritanical and the incarnational. As much as they would like to escape from and even eliminate theology, the new atheists' contemporary joust with Christian faith is part of a long, internal, and inescapably theological affair.

According to most contemporary Christian theologians, in any case, we cannot hope to encounter God by evading all specific times, particular places, and actual experiences. God is not a hypothesis that can be abstracted from entanglement with the contingencies of natural and human history. Dawkins's goal of deciding the God question scientifically by turning God into a hypothesis is as blatant an expression of cognitional puritanism as were the ancient gnostic efforts to arrive at pure knowledge of God by first denying the incarnation. But the deeply incarnate Christian God cannot be encountered in a dualistically sterilized cognitive space sealed off from concrete events, images, symbols, and metaphors that arise from culturally, geographically, and historically contingent experiences of actual people. Puritans, whether religious, scientific, or moral, are embarrassed that what is most perfect would become so contaminated by contact with contingency and perishability. But this is exactly the kind of perfection that the self-emptying God of Christian faith represents.

To Hitchens and Harris the fact that faith is accompanied by images of God at all makes Christianity intellectually worthless. This puritanical intolerance of any God whose reality becomes known through images carries over to their reading of the Bible. In an exceptional display of cognitional, ethical, and exegetical abstemiousness, Hitchens and Harris interpret the wide variety of biblical styles and genres as evidence of unacceptable scholarship on the part of God. I have already mentioned Harris's shock that if the Bible was written by God it should have its science and math straight. For Hitchens the discrepancies between different accounts of Jesus' birth and crucifixion in the Gospels are already enough to overthrow the doctrine of biblical inspiration. How could an omniscient deity possibly have been the guiding light behind all that textual sloppiness, not to mention the misleading cosmology? I was frankly surprised that our expert interpreters forgot to flog Luke and Matthew for plagiarizing Mark and the Gospel source known as Q. Why should God be allowed to get by without footnotes? Why isn't there more sheer learnedness if the Bible is an inspired book? I could go on and on, but I assume the point has been made.

## EVOLUTION AND CHRISTIAN THEOLOGY

The puritanical premise that leads Dawkins to reject Christianity on moral grounds also underlies his belief that the Christian

God must be rejected on scientific grounds as well. Darwin's picture of life, according to Dawkins, demolishes the God of the Bible decisively.[9] How so? Evolutionary science shows that nature exhibits no sign of intelligent design. Dawkins wants a universe that fits his idea of engineering elegance and perfect design, just as he wants a God who corresponds to his notion of moral perfection. He gets neither. Therefore, for Dawkins, God simply cannot exist. A perfectly good God would never have made a world in which so much evolutionary struggle, waste, suffering, and death take place. If God were a perfect engineer, there would be no room for the imperfections biologists find in the organic world.

Here, then, the puritanical view of morality characteristic of the new atheism finds its parallel in a perfectionistic model of divine creation in which God should have created the world in a finished and finalized state once and for all in the beginning. Either the God of the Bible must be a perfect moral role model and a perfect engineer, or else this God is not permitted by Dawkins to exist at all.

But to Christian faith Dawkins's species of perfectionism, both moral and cosmic, is a dead end. If the universe were finished instantaneously, where could it go from there? Maybe, then, there is a good theological reason that a God who wants the universe to have an open future would put up with imperfection and ambiguity. If you don't like a world in which either suicide bombers or evolutionary monstrosities are permitted to exist, a good mental experiment is to imagine what it would be like to exist in the perfectly designed universe idealized by the new atheists and their creationist forebears. In keeping with their biblical literalism, the universe they want would have to have been finished to perfection on the first day of creation. An instantaneously completed initial act of divine prestidigitation would guarantee that there would be no suffering, no evil, and no need for the creation to evolve into something different over immensely long periods of time. In their instructions as to how a decent God should act, the new atheists demand that either the world be finished once and for all in the beginning, or else there is no role for God to play at all. A morally acceptable God would get things completely right from day one. The universe would be an unblemished, unchanging reflection of its divine engineer. There would be no growing pains, no death, no terrorists. There would be no theodicy problem either, since there would be no evil to reconcile with the existence of God.

Neither, of course, would there be any life, any freedom, any future, any adventure, any grand cosmic story, any opening to infinite horizons up ahead. Nor would there be the opportunity for each of us to develop character and practice virtue. The problem with the new atheists' magical ideal of creation—one that they seem to have borrowed once again from creationists and ID theists—is that creation would have nowhere to go. Locked eternally into splendid perfection, the universe would allow no room for indeterminacy, accidents, or freedom. Every last detail would be frozen into its destined position from the beginning; human beings, if one can imagine them existing at all, would be puppets and statues.

Only a still unfinished universe—such as the one that geology, cosmology, and biology have been revealing to us over the past two centuries—could provide the setting for human freedom and creativity. Of course, to say that the universe is "unfinished" is to imply that it is imperfect, ambiguous, and open to tragic as well as marvelous outcomes. Even the fact that religions themselves are so imperfect, and sometimes horrifically evil, is completely consistent with the fact that they too are part of an unfinished universe. It is important to face up to the evils associated with religious faiths, and on this score the new atheists are right to point them out. At the same time, though, it is hard to imagine how a Creator who truly loves freedom, diversity, and novelty could ever have rounded everything off presto into a closed and static circle of eternal sameness. An initially perfect universe would be deadly.

The shadow side of any unfinished, and hence imperfect, universe is ambiguity and evil, including the poison in our religions. Understandably we long for a world without evil, and so it is appropriate to hope for the eventual fulfillment of our lives and the whole universe. The Christian hope is for a universe in which evil will be conquered and all tears will be wiped away. Such a hope, by setting forth the possibility of a new future, is a great incentive to moral action. But we need to be very careful about what we ask for as far as the past and present state of the universe is concerned. An initially perfect design, which is what Dawkins asks for—otherwise he would not be so cynical about God's failure as an engineer—would mean the end of evolution before it even began. And perfectionism, both moral and scientific, would mean the end of hope. Perfectionism is a sure way to close off the future and prevent the world and our lives from ever becoming new.

As the ultimate ground of novelty, freedom, and hope, the Christian God offers the entire universe as well as ourselves the opportunity of ongoing liberation from the lifelessness of perfect design. Evolution, therefore, may be understood, at a theological level, as the story of the world's gradual emergence from initial chaos and monotony, and of its adventurous search for more intensely elaborate modes of being. The God of evolution humbly invites creatures to participate in the ongoing creation of the universe. This gracious invitation to share in the creation of the universe is consistent with the fundamental Christian belief that the ultimate ground of the universe and our own lives is the loving, vulnerable, defenseless, and self-emptying generosity of God.

# Suggestions for Further Reading

Haught, John F. *What Is God? How to Think about the Divine.* New York: Paulist Press, 1986.

McGrath, Alister E. *Dawkins' God: Genes, Memes, and the Meaning of Life.* Malden, Mass.: Blackwell Publishing, 2005.

———. *The Twilight of Atheism: The Rise and Fall of Disbelief in the Modern World.* New York: Doubleday, 2004.

Ward, Keith. *God: A Guide for the Perplexed.* Oxford: Oneworld Publications, 2003.

———. *Is Religion Dangerous?* Grand Rapids: Wm. B. Eerdmans, 2007.

# Notes

## Introduction

1. Richard Dawkins, *The God Delusion* (New York: Houghton Mifflin, 2006); Sam Harris, *The End of Faith: Religion, Terror, and the Future of Reason* (New York: W. W. Norton & Co., 2004); and *Letter to a Christian Nation* (New York: Knopf, 2007); Christopher Hitchens, *God Is Not Great: How Religion Poisons Everything* (New York: Hachette Book Group USA, 2007).

2. Victor J. Stenger, *God: The Failed Hypothesis: How Science Shows That God Does Not Exist* (Amherst, N.Y.: Prometheus Books, 2007); Carl Sagan, *The Demon-Haunted World: Science as a Candle in the Dark* (New York: Ballantine Books, 1997); Steven Weinberg, *Dreams of a Final Theory* (New York: Pantheon, 1992); Michael Shermer, *How We Believe: The Search for God in an Age of Science* (New York: W. H. Freeman, 2000); Owen Flanagan, *The Problem of the Soul: Two Visions of Mind and How to Reconcile Them* (New York: Basic Books, 2002).

3. Daniel Dennett, *Breaking the Spell: Religion as a Natural Phenomenon* (New York: Viking, 2006).

4. See n. 2 above.

## Chapter 1: How New Is the New Atheism?

1. I recommend that readers look also at Harris's "Atheist Manifesto" online at http://www.truthdig.com/dig/item/200512_an_atheist_manifesto/ (accessed October 14, 2007).

2. Page numbers refer to Harris's *End of Faith* unless otherwise indicated.

3. Hitchens, *God Is Not Great*; Dawkins, *God Delusion*. Page numbers for these authors refer to these books, unless otherwise noted.

4. Jacques Monod, *Chance and Necessity: An Essay on the Natural Philosophy of Modern Biology*, trans. Austryn Wainhouse (New York: Vintage Books, 1972), 160–80.

5. William James, *The Will to Believe and Other Essays in Popular Philosophy* (New York: Dover Publications, 1956).

6. Phillip E. Johnson, *Darwin on Trial* (Washington, D.C.: Regnery Gateway, 1991).

7. Edwin Abbott, *Flatland: A Romance of Many Dimensions* (Amherst, N.Y.: Prometheus Books, 2005).

## Chapter 2: How Atheistic Is the New Atheism?

1. Sam Harris, "Rational Mysticism," http://www.secularhumanism .org/index.php?section=library&page=harris_25_6 (accessed October 14, 2007).

2. Sigmund Freud, *The Future of an Illusion,* trans. James Strachey (New York: W. W. Norton & Co., 1961), 69.

3. Richard Dawkins, "Tanner Lecture on Human Values" at Harvard University, November 19 and 20, 2003, cited by *Science and Theology News* online, http://www.stnews.org/archives/2004_february/web_x_ richard.html.

4. Harris (205–207) attempts to explain what happiness is, but while his writing is mostly crisp and clear, his ideas on happiness are extremely obscure.

5. Jean-Paul Sartre, *The Words* (New York: Vintage Books, 1981), 247.

6. I take up the question of morality and religious faith in chap. 6.

7. Friedrich Nietzsche, *The Gay Science,* ed. Walter Kaufmann (New York: Vintage Books, 1974), 181–82.

8. Harris, "Rational Mysticism."

9. Nietzsche, *Gay Science*, 181–82.

10. Jean-Paul Sartre, *Existentialism Is a Humanism*, trans. Carol Macomber (New Haven, Conn.: Yale University Press, 1970).

11. See Schubert Ogden, *The Reality of God and Other Essays* (New York: Harper & Row, 1977).

## Chapter 3: Does Theology Matter?

1. An *Edge* Discussion of *Beyond Belief:* Science, Religion, Reason, and Survival, Salk Institute, La Jolla, California, November 5–7, 2006; http://www.edge.org/discourse/bb.html (accessed October 18, 2007).

2. Cited in *Discoveries and Opinions of Galileo,* trans. with Introduction and notes by Stillman Drake (New York: Anchor Books, 1957), 186–87.

3. Ibid., 187.

4. Daniel Dennett, as interviewed in John Brockman, *The Third Culture* (New York: Touchstone Books, 1996), 187.

5. A good example is Charles Davis, *Temptations of Religion* (New York: Harper & Row, 1973).

## Chapter 4: Is God a Hypothesis?

1. Harris, "Atheist Manifesto."

2. Robert Bellah, *Beyond Belief: Essays on Religion in a Post-traditional World* (New York: Harper & Row, 1970), 254.

3. Flanagan, *Problem of the Soul*, 167–68.

4. Victor Stenger, a physicist and less hostile proponent of the "new atheism," has written a book with the title *God: The Failed Hypothesis: How Science Shows That God Does Not Exist*. As the title makes clear, this book adds little to the claim of Dawkins that I am examining in this chapter, and my criticism of Dawkins applies to Stenger as well.

5. Dennett, *Breaking the Spell*, 21, 55. Dennett denies that "bright" signifies superiority, but clearly he is underestimating the power of language.

6. See Michael Buckley, *At the Origins of Modern Atheism* (New Haven, Conn.: Yale University Press, 1987).

7. Holmes Rolston III, *Science and Religion: A Critical Survey* (New York: Random House, 1987), 336.

8. Charles Darwin, letter to W. Graham, July 3, 1881, in *The Life and Letters of Charles Darwin,* ed. Francis Darwin (New York: Basic Books, 1959), 285.

9. For an extended discussion see my book *Is Nature Enough? Meaning and Truth in the Age of Science* (Cambridge: Cambridge University Press, 2006).

## Chapter 5: Why Do People Believe?

1. See also Dennett, *Breaking the Spell*, 3–115.

2. Shermer, *How We Believe.*

3. Robert Hinde, *Why Gods Persist: A Scientific Approach to Religions* (New York: Routledge, 1999).

4. E. O. Wilson, *Consilience: The Unity of Knowledge* (New York: Knopf, 1998); Pascal Boyer, *Religion Explained: The Evolutionary Origins of Religious Thought* (New York: Basic Books, 2001); Scott Atran, *In Gods We Trust: The Evolutionary Landscape of Religion* (New York: Oxford University Press, 2002).

5. George C. Williams, *Adaptation and Natural Selection: A Critique of Some Current Evolutionary Thought* (Princeton, N.J.: Princeton University Press, 1996); William D. Hamilton, "The Genetical Evolution of Social Behavior," *Journal of Theoretical Biology* 7 (1964): 1–52; John Maynard Smith, *The Evolution of Sex* (New York: Cambridge University Press, 1978); Robert L. Trivers, *Social Evolution* (Menlo Park, Calif.: Benjamin Cummings, 1985); Richard D. Alexander, *Darwinism and Human Affairs* (Seattle: University of Washington Press, 1979).

6. Boyer, *Religion Explained.*

7. Ibid., 145.

8. Ibid., 137–67.

9. Dennett's discussion of memes can be found in *Breaking the Spell,* 341–57.

10. See my *God after Darwin: A Theology of Evolution,* 2nd ed. (Boulder, Colo.: Westview Press, 2007), and *Deeper Than Darwin: The Prospect for Religion in the Age of Evolution* (Boulder, Colo.: Westview Press, 2003).

11. I am thinking especially of the many works of Michael Ruse, whose writings are models of calmness, fairness, and scholarship. See, for example, his *Darwin and Design: Does Evolution Have a Purpose?* (Cambridge, Mass.: Harvard University Press, 2003).

12. See Loyal Rue, *By the Grace of Guile: The Role of Deception in Natural History and Human Affairs* (New York: Oxford University Press, 1994). Rue, himself a professor of religious studies, sometimes refers to religious illusions as "lies."

13. The tenets of scientific naturalism are summarized in this book's Introduction.

14. See especially Paul Tillich, *Dynamics of Faith* (New York: Harper Torchbooks, 1958).

15. Daniel Dennett refers fleetingly to Tillich, but exhibits no evidence of understanding or studying this theologian. See *Breaking the Spell,* 166, 191, 163.

16. For a deeper development of this theological perspective see my book *Is Nature Enough? Meaning and Truth in the Age of Science* (Cambridge: Cambridge University Press, 2006).

## Chapter 6: Can We Be Good without God?

1. Alfred North Whitehead, *Science and the Modern World* (New York: Free Press, 1967), 191.

2. Søren Kierkegaard, *The Sickness unto Death,* trans. Howard V. Hong and Edna H. Hong (Princeton, N.J.: Princeton University Press, 1983), 82.

3. See also Matt Ridley, *The Origins of Virtue: Human Instincts and the Evolution of Cooperation* (New York: Penguin Books, 1998).

4. See Robert Wright, *The Moral Animal: Evolutionary Psychology and Everyday Life* (New York: Pantheon Books, 1994).

5. Ridley, *Origins of Virtue,* 12.

6. Paul Tillich, *A History of Christian Thought* (New York: Simon & Schuster, 1969), 264.

7. For a more expanded development of this point see my book *Is Nature Enough?*

## Chapter 7: Is God Personal?

1. Albert Einstein, *Ideas and Opinions* (New York: Bonanza Books, 1954), 11.

2. Ibid.

3. For example, Ursula Goodenough, *The Sacred Depths of Nature* (New York: Oxford University Press, 1998); Chet Raymo, *Skeptics and True Believers: The Exhilarating Connection between Science and Religion* (New York: Walker & Co., 1998).

4. Steven Weinberg, *Dreams of a Final Theory: The Search for the Fundamental Laws of Nature* (New York: Pantheon Books, 1992), 245.

5. Ibid., 241–61.

6. Ibid., 256.

7. Here I refer the reader to my books on evolution and theology: *God after Darwin* and *Deeper Than Darwin.*

8. Percival Davis and Dean H. Kenyon, *Of Pandas and People: The Central Question of Biological Origins,* 2nd ed. (Dallas: Haughton Publishing Co., 1993).

9. See Ullica Segerstråle, *Defenders of the Truth: The Battle for Science in the Sociobiology Debate and Beyond* (New York: Oxford University Press, 2000), 399–400.

## Chapter 8: Christian Theology and the New Atheism

1. Søren Kierkegaard, "The Sickness unto Death," in *Fear and Trembling and the Sickness unto Death,* trans. Walter Lowrie (Garden City, N.Y.: Doubleday Anchor Books, 1954), 218.

2. Pope John Paul II, *Fides et Ratio*, encyclical letter, September 14, 1998; http://www.ewtn.com/library/ENCYC/JP2FIDES.HTM (accessed October 14, 2007).

3. Here I recommend Daniel Maguire's *The Moral Core of Judaism and Christianity: Reclaiming the Revolution* (Minneapolis: Fortress Press, 1993).

4. Online at: http://almaz.com/nobel/peace/MLK-jail.html.

5. Actually scientism is also an offshoot of dualistic mythology, but I cannot develop the point here.

6. Support for my suggestion comes especially from Paul Ricoeur, *The Symbolism of Evil*, trans. Emerson Buchanan (Boston: Beacon Press, 1969).

7. See Charles Hartshorne, *The Divine Relativity* (New Haven, Conn.: Yale University Press, 1948); and Schubert Ogden, *The Reality of God and Other Essays* (New York: Harper & Row, 1977), 1–70.

8. When I use the expression "dominant themes" here, I mean "dominant" from the point of view of countless Christian theologians whom the new atheists ignore completely. Of course, not every theologian or biblical scholar would emphasize the themes of liberation, promise, hope, kenosis, and incarnation in the way I am doing here. But here I am following, for example, the approach of Jürgen Moltmann, who cannot separate the ideas of promise, liberation, and hope from the biblical idea of God. See his book *The Spirit of Life: A Universal Affirmation*, trans. Margaret Kohl (Minneapolis: Fortress Press, 1992).

9. Richard Dawkins, *The Blind Watchmaker* (New York: W. W. Norton & Co., 1986); and *River out of Eden* (New York: Basic Books, 1995).

# Index